The United Nations

Look for these and other books in the Lucent Overview series:

The United Nations

by Adam Woog

LUCENT
B·O·O·K·S

LUCENT *Overview Series*

LUCENT *Overview Series*

Library of Congress Cataloging-in-Publication Data

Woog, Adam, 1953-
    The United Nations / by Adam Woog
        p.   cm. — (Lucent overview series)
    Includes bibliographical references and index.
    Summary: Discusses the founding of the United Nations, its peacekeeping, economic, social, and environmental roles, and possibilities for the future.
    ISBN 1-56006-145-6 (alk. paper)
    1. United Nations—Juvenile literature. [1. United Nations.]
I. Title. II. Series.
JX1977.Z8W665   1993
341.23—dc20   93-3767
                                                    CIP
                                                      AC

Copyright © 1994 by Lucent Books, Inc.
P.O. Box 289011, San Diego, CA 92198-9011
Printed in the U.S.A.

Contents

Introduction

SINCE 1945 THE United Nations has been, directly or indirectly, part of the lives of virtually everyone on earth. It has been praised, ridiculed, condemned, and ignored. It has been used for both positive and negative goals. It has often fallen short of its main purposes—to provide global peace and security and to deliver humanitarian aid and disaster relief to those in need. It has also, on occasion, been accused of being out-of-date, a useless relic crippled by bureaucracy and waste. In a world characterized until recently by two rival superpowers flanked by respective allies and neutral countries, the UN has often been paralyzed.

But the world is changing fast. It is no longer torn apart by a world war and witnessing the growth of new superpowers as it was when the UN was born. The Soviet Union has disappeared almost overnight, and the cold war is, for all intents and purposes, finished.

Although many small, regional wars are still being fought, the immediate threat of world war has been replaced by new challenges. The new "weapons" are cultural imports—in the form of movies, books, and music—and economic competition. Ancient ethnic blood feuds coexist with a modern, electronic global village. The world population is larger but the world itself seems smaller.

The changes now taking place hold the

(Opposite page) A Norwegian soldier, a member of the United Nations peacekeeping force deployed in southern Lebanon in 1978, scans the countryside. Since 1945 the UN has provided security, humanitarian aid, and disaster relief to those in need around the world.

7

promise of a new beginning for the UN, and its challenge for the future is to fit into this quickly changing world. Secretary-General Boutros Boutros-Ghali introduced provocative proposals to give the UN real power and to fulfill, after forty years, the organization's original promise of world peace—a promise that the world has cherished for centuries.

The UN is uniquely equipped to bring about world peace. Its resources extend around the globe and it commands the attention of world leaders. Boutros-Ghali has written that no other organization

> can match the United Nation's global network of information-gathering and constructive activity, which reaches from modern world centers of power down to the villages and families where people carry out the irreducible [smallest] responsibilities of their lives. At the other end of the scale, only the United Nations can convene global-scale meetings of ministers and heads of state or governments to examine complex issues and propose integrated approaches.

Hundreds of representatives from countries around the globe gather in 1992 for the opening of the forty-seventh session of the UN General Assembly.

Malnourished children in Somalia eagerly await their share of milk, donated by the UN. The UN routinely supplies such humanitarian aid to needy people worldwide.

These complex issues reflect a close interweaving and interdependence of economic, social, and political factors. Former Secretary-General Javier Pérez de Cuéllar, in a 1987 report to the UN General Assembly, wrote:

> The symbiosis [interdependence] of development, environment and population is beginning to be appreciated. We know that the remedy for drug abuse must be composed of many elements, economic, social, and legal. Arms limitation efforts are hampered in some areas by social and economic factors that frequently invite violence and instability, as well as by political tensions.

This book discusses a number of timeless themes that have challenged the UN since it began. Though the details change continually, the larger issues seem always to remain the same. The challenges of achieving peace, prosperity, and health for all the world's people have not diminished with time. If anything, they have grown larger, with dramatic new developments occurring daily. In a small way this reflects the challenge that lies ahead for the men and women who work for the UN. They are striving to make our world a better one, even as it changes.

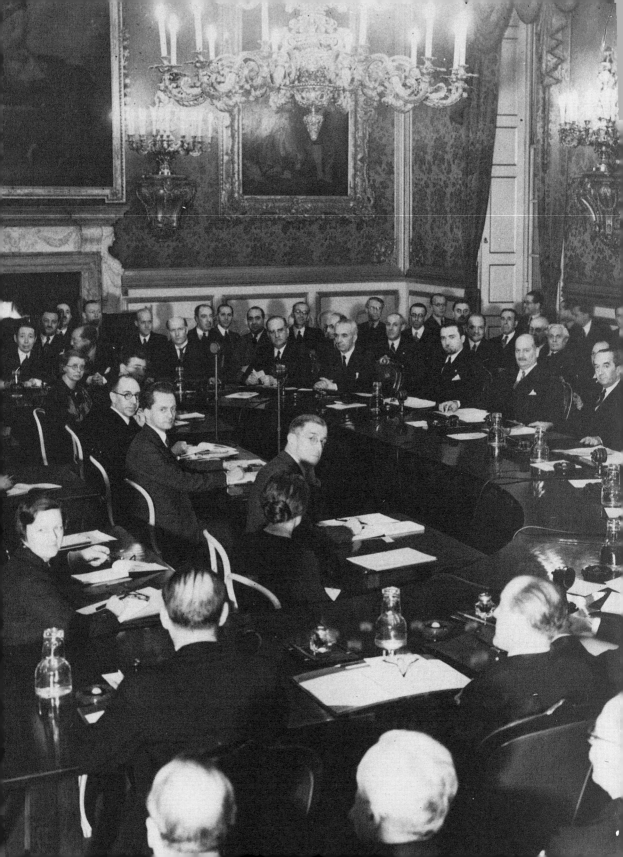

1

The Road to the United Nations

Those who cannot remember the past are condemned to repeat it.
—George Santayana, *Life of Reason*

THE THREAT OF war has existed as long as humans have lived. Sometimes that threat erupts into war itself. Any of a variety of issues—border disputes, ethnic clashes, greed over resources—can trigger a war. Some parts of the world, such as Ireland or the Middle East, have been in a nearly continuous state of conflict for hundreds or even thousands of years.

But there is another side of the coin. When we witness enough war, we are moved to create peace. Several major attempts have been made in modern history to form a lasting peace. As journalist George Slocombe noted at the end of World War I, "After each great war the idea of a federation of the nations and of perpetual peace [has] appeared like the Biblical vision of God moving upon the face of the waters."

Given the complexity of world politics this has never been an easy task, or one assured of success. Still, the creation of the United Nations following the worst conflict in history, World War

(Opposite page) The League of Nations meets in 1936 as the world edges closer to a second global war. The league, like the Congress of Vienna before it, could not fulfill the hope and promise of world peace.

11

II, reflected the hopes and dreams of a world that never wanted to see war again.

Two conferences that preceded the UN shared its underlying theme of permanent, global peace: the Congress of Vienna, held in 1815 after the Napoleonic Wars, and the post-World War I Paris Peace Conference of 1919, which resulted in the formation of the League of Nations.

The Napoleonic Wars

For a time Napoleon Bonaparte was the most powerful ruler in the world. After seizing the French throne in 1799, he tried to bring all of Europe under his rule. The result was a long and bloody war. The number of French military casualties alone in the Napoleonic Wars has been estimated at half a million.

At its peak Napoleon's empire covered much of Europe. But Napoleon was unsuccessful in bringing some countries, particularly England and Russia, under his control. In 1812 he mounted a major campaign against Russia, sending his *Grande Armée* ("large army")—the largest army ever—to conquer Moscow.

The mission was a disaster, and Napoleon was forced to retreat without a victory. The bitter cold of an early winter added to his casualties, and fewer than ten thousand of Napoleon's half-million soldiers were fit for combat by the time they reached home. The Quadruple Alliance (Austria, Russia, Prussia, and England) forced the broken leader to abdicate, or step down, and restored the former king, Louis XVIII, to power in France.

The Congress of Vienna

The need to create order in Europe was crucial in the following months. The result was the Congress of Vienna of 1815, the biggest peace conference the world had yet seen. Although it

Napoleon Bonaparte, perhaps one of the most powerful rulers the world has known, tried to bring all of Europe under his control.

concerned only European nations, it can be considered the first major global meeting concerned with peace.

Hopes ran high for the conference. As Archduke John of Austria, a delegate to the congress, noted in his diary: "Oh, if I could but transmit to every one what I feel! Then Europe would have peace for a long time [and] forget, abandon the lust for possession and ambition. Mankind has suffered cruelly; it is time to help it."

Frivolity often mixed with the congress's real work. The presence of hundreds of delegates and their entourages, or attendants, created an excuse for an endless series of masked balls, hunts, concerts, and other diversions. This social activity laid the congress open to charges of uselessness. One of the delegates, Charles Joseph, prince de Ligne, remarked that "the Congress dances but accomplishes nothing."

There was also a good deal of petty bickering and fussing over protocol, or rules of conduct. Nearly as much time was spent deciding who would enter rooms first, or where delegates would sit, as on real work. At one point the Spanish ambassador took offense because the French ambassador's carriage was ahead of his on the way to a function. The Spaniard ordered his driver to push the Frenchman's coach out of the way. A street brawl ensued that very nearly caused both nations to sever diplomatic ties.

Reforms

Still, much genuine good was accomplished. The congress introduced reforms that led to nearly one hundred years of peace in Europe. Just as importantly, it inspired long-term attempts, by statesmen and ordinary citizens, to create organizations dedicated to the creation of a single world

An engraving depicts the historic gathering of delegates from across Europe at the Congress of Vienna in 1815. It can be considered the first global meeting concerned with peace.

government. By solidifying among these groups a theme of international cooperation, the congress was a direct influence on the later formation of the League of Nations and the UN.

One concrete achievement was the issuance of statements condemning such practices as anti-Semitism and the international slave trade. These marked an important milestone in cooperation between countries on human rights issues. Another success was in restoring, as closely as possible, national boundaries that had been split by Napoleon's empire.

Failures

Still, the congress failed in one respect—to establish a permanent peace. In part this was because the delegates ignored two powerful, connected ideas that were then sweeping Europe. The first was democratic rule by the common people, and the second was national rule based on ethnic or cultural similarities. These ideas would in later years become crucial to the formation of the League of Nations and the UN.

Democracy had caught on before—in ancient Greece and during the French Revolution—and by the time the congress convened it was being tested again across the Atlantic in a new country called the United States of America. But the Congress of Vienna ignored it, emphasizing instead the restoration of power to royal families. Writing at the time of the Paris conference that created the League of Nations, diplomat Harry Hansen underscored this difference:

> Vienna was a congress of princes and arbitrary rulers. The hereditary overlords decided according to their aims and ambitions, in a spirit of greed and selfishness, [but] the men who meet at [the Paris Peace Conference] have before them [the consent of the governed and] the last 100 years of progress toward democratic government.

An artist depicts a scene from the French Revolution, where democratic ideals took hold early. Despite the gaining popularity of democracy, the Congress of Vienna emphasized the restoration of power to Europe's royal families.

Struggles for various ethnic groups to gain freedom had been raging all across Europe long before the Vienna congress convened. Since the congress restored national boundaries to their old lines, with little regard for ethnic or cultural considerations, these freedom movements continued to grow dramatically in the years following the congress.

In his book *The Congress of Vienna,* Sir Charles Webster notes that the delegates' loyalty to the ruling families was a reflection of the times:

> Accusation on this score must, in fact, be levelled against the age as a whole and not against the statesmen. . . . Yet it cannot be asserted that the statesmen concerned were equal to the opportunity presented to them. They were limited in outlook, too prone to compromise, lacking in faith and courage. None . . . made any attempt to do more than the obvious. They were content with expedients [quick solutions].

Still another factor in the congress's failure was an inability to control arms buildups by the victorious nations. England, for instance, was determined to keep its superiority on the seas, and Prussia was still extremely proud of its large army. Occasional flareups among these powerful countries continued on a small scale even after the congress, especially in those parts of the world, such as Africa, that were being colonized by Europeans.

World War I

Tension continued to mount in Europe as the years went on, until in 1914 the most destructive war the world had ever seen finally broke out. Some ten million soldiers and an equal number of civilians died in World War I. Twenty million

French soldiers drive back German forces in France during World War I. Despite efforts to create peace in Europe, tensions mounted, and in 1914 World War I broke out.

were wounded, and another twenty million died of famine and disease. Although the battles took place in Europe, this was the first war to have truly global consequences. The cost in human lives and property and the spread of war-related disease and famine had an impact on the world for years to come.

The war itself was caused by many factors. Chief among them were the hostile actions of Germany, the most powerful military force in Europe, and its ambitious ally, Austria-Hungary. Rivalry between Germany and England over superiority on the seas, as well as disagreement over colonial Africa, helped build tension. Europe smoldered, ready to burst into flames at any moment.

Another factor was the same one that had long plagued Europe: the struggle between royal dynasties and those who favored democracy. The most serious of these struggles was brewing in the Balkan region of Eastern Europe. While ethnic groups in several small states (including Serbia, Bosnia, and Herzegovina) sought independence from the Ottoman Empire, Austria-Hungary was expanding its power into the region.

Diplomats called the Balkans "the Eastern problem." If Europe was a smoldering fire, then the Eastern problem was gasoline poured on top. The match that finally set everything aflame was a single action: the assassination of Archduke Francis Ferdinand, heir to the Austrian throne, in the Bosnian town of Sarajevo in 1914.

"One peace"

Austria-Hungary and Germany declared war on Serbia. Against them, joining together in aid to Serbia, were several countries including Russia, England, France, Belgium, Japan, Italy, and the United States; collectively, this group was

Archduke Francis Ferdinand and his wife Sophie leave the Senate House in Sarajevo, Bosnia. Five minutes after this photograph was taken they were assassinated. The assassination triggered the start of World War I.

known as the Allies. The nations of the world understood that they could not stand by; in the words of the French statesman Aristide Briand, "There is not one peace for America, nor one peace for Europe, one peace for Africa, but only one peace for the entire world."

The war lasted for four long years. In the end, the Allies won through a combination of factors, including the civilian resistance in France and Russia, the power (in troops, manufacturing, and naval superiority) of the British, and the late entry of the United States in 1917, which provided a major boost in manpower, hardware, and moral support.

The end of the war was marked by the signing of an armistice, or truce, at the palace of Versailles, near Paris, in November 1918. This was followed, early the next year, by the largest peace conference since the Congress of Vienna. Delegates to the Paris talks had three immediate problems: deciding the fate of Germany, redefining the borders of the European countryside, and providing aid to war-torn nations. But they also wanted to form a long-range approach to peace, and American president Woodrow Wilson formed a committee within the conference to create an organization—the League of Nations—that could address such a global concern.

The plan was met with enthusiasm by many. Citizens' peace groups (such as the American League to Enforce Peace, one of whose founders was former president William Taft) had become increasingly active and influential during the war. In a speech in 1916 Taft had declared, "The nations of the world have become each others' neighbors. It is to their interests that they should understand each other."

A draft proposal

Wilson was adamantly in favor of making the league a democratic organization. No more, he

Government leaders meet in Versailles, France, for the signing of the peace treaty that ended World War I. After four years of brutal fighting, the Allied powers emerged victorious.

President Woodrow Wilson was instrumental in forming the League of Nations. He envisioned the league as a democratic organization that could address the global concern of developing a long-range approach to peace.

felt, would the world tolerate totalitarian government. Speaking before the U.S. Congress in 1917, he had stated:

> No representative of any self-governed nation will [attempt] such covenants of selfishness and compromise as were entered into at the Congress of Vienna. The thought of the plain people here and everywhere throughout the world, the people who enjoy no privilege and have very simple and unsophisticated standards of right and wrong, is the air all governments must henceforth breathe if they would live.

Three months after the Paris talks convened, Wilson's committee had prepared a draft proposal, which they called the Covenant of the League of Nations. Much of its framework was the work of the South African farmer-statesman-soldier, Gen. Jan Smuts, who had capped a distinguished military career by becoming an influential advocate for peace. Smuts's pamphlet, *The League of Nations: A Practical Suggestion*—written in the summer of 1918, before the end of the war—formed the basis for Wilson's plan. Its spirit was summarized by General Smuts when he urged "pity and restraint" toward the defeated

Gen. Jan Smuts's pamphlet, The League of Nations: A Practical Suggestion, *called for "pity and restraint" toward defeated nations and provided the basis for Wilson's ideas about the league.*

nations, rather than punishing them. As he put it, "Civilization is one body and . . . we are all members, one of another."

Balancing interests

Wilson and his colleagues suggested that a logical headquarters for the new organization would be Geneva, the largest city in Switzerland. Switzerland had remained neutral during the war, and Geneva had long been the home of such peace-oriented organizations as the International Red Cross. Although headquartered in Europe, the league was to be worldwide in composition—the first organization of its kind to include an Asian nation, Japan, and a North American nation, the United States, as permanent members of its highest council.

The league's primary goal would be to solve international disputes through discussion, not armed conflict. Membership would be open to all nations except those defeated in the war; these members would be sworn to standards of security, disarmament, open diplomacy, and economic and social cooperation. The first weapon in settling disputes would be arbitration—that is, discussion and compromise. If this failed, economic sanctions—the breaking of trade ties with an aggressive country—would be the next step. Armed conflict would be tolerated only as a last resort.

A key element in the covenant was the stipulation that the league would not maintain its own armed troops. The league would thus have little real power beyond that of moral or economic persuasion. As Sir Eric Drummond, the league's first secretary-general, said in a speech before the British House of Commons, "The League of Nations may give occasional assistance, frequent assistance, effective assistance; but the League of Nations is not, and cannot be, a complete instrument for bringing order out of chaos." Still, the delegates believed—or wanted to believe—that

The League of Nations headquarters in Geneva, Switzerland. Geneva was chosen because Switzerland had long been home to peace-oriented organizations and because the country had remained neutral during the war.

Sir Eric Drummond, the league's first secretary-general. Drummond and the delegates proceeded with the hope that aggressive nations would abide by the league's decisions. In reality, the league had little power.

aggressive nations would abide by the league's decisions, and plans went ahead for its formation.

The covenant was, at best, a compromise document, written by delegates trying to balance their nations' interests with those of the world as a whole. The results were mixed, but, as King Albert of Belgium remarked at the time, "What would you have? They did what they could." The final document failed to satisfy extreme pacifists, who rejected all forms of force, as well as extreme internationalists, who supported cooperation between nations and wanted the league to have its own army and to act as a global enforcer. Still, a majority of the nations at the conference signed the document.

Rejection

But the league was doomed to failure almost from the very beginning. Ironically, the reason was largely that the United States, the country of the man who had done the most to promote it, refused to join.

After the war the mood across America was one of isolationism. The country was still recovering, and a majority of citizens were unwilling to risk getting entangled again in faraway disputes. Wilson lobbied hard to change this attitude, criss-crossing the country and making speeches such as one in which he stated:

> Unless you get the united, concerted purpose and power of the great governments of the world behind this settlement, it will fall down like a house of cards. There is only one power to put behind the liberation of mankind, and that is the power of mankind. It is the power of the united moral forces of the world.

But Congress, responding to the prevailing mood of isolationism, rejected the covenant and refused to join the League of Nations.

The league's basic premise was to enforce its

President Wilson addresses a crowd in Tacoma, Washington, where he urges support for the League of Nations. His passionate appeal for American participation in the league failed to sway the U.S. Congress.

rulings through economic sanctions—a premise that was worthless once the United States, the most powerful trading partner in the world, failed to cooperate. Despite this rebuff, the league became a reality and continued to perform limited work for the next twenty-five years. Although it never became a major political force, in some ways it performed admirably. It represented, for example, the first instance of democratic cooperation's taking hold on an international scale. Any country could come before the general assembly to discuss problems and concerns. And its suborganizations, such as those dealing with issues of labor, law, communications, and health, served as models for later UN groups.

The league also helped perfect the art of "quiet diplomacy," those informal, casual meetings that take place between top diplomats away from the pressures of the public spotlight. Sir Robert Vansittart, a senior British diplomat, once remarked that "if Monsieur A. has Herr B. and Signor C. to

The first meeting of the League of Nations, November 15, 1920. Despite its failure to become a major political force and fulfill its goal of worldwide peace, the league continued for twenty-five years.

dinner—even a bad dinner—several times a year, the tone of the diplomatic correspondence between [them] undergoes a change. Before the war, this curious and general trait was never properly exploited."

"War everywhere"

Still, the league never fulfilled its initial promise of providing peace. Indeed, small wars were breaking out even before the Paris conference had ended. Gen. Sir Henry Wilson, then the chief of Britain's Imperial General Staff, remarked in 1920 that "this Peace Treaty has resulted in war everywhere."

The potential for larger conflicts also loomed. Germany was more or less intact after the war, but the new countries that had been created around it, such as Czechoslovakia and Yugoslavia, were small and weak; they also contained large numbers of German minorities, and the combination made the smaller countries vulnerable. As historian Sally Marks notes, "On the whole, the peacemakers at Paris . . . assumed erroneously that Germany would abide by their decisions and accept her new neighbors."

Although the league's covenant called for a reduction of arms, Great Britain and France were the only nations to seriously disarm. Germany also began failing in its promise to make war reparations, or repayments, to its victims, and the league was reluctant to discipline Germany. This failure, combined with runaway inflation in Germany, helped pave the way for the rise of Hitler and the Nazi party in the 1920s and 1930s.

The league failed also in the Mediterranean. The dictator Benito Mussolini had gained power in Italy and was becoming bolder in his demands for world attention. When Italy and Greece came into armed conflict over the strategic island of

Corfu in 1923, the league did nothing more than issue a statement saying that "measures of coercion" (specifically, Italy's bombing of the island) did not necessarily constitute an act of war. In the words of historian Marks, "The League had failed its first test."

Germany was admitted to the League of Nations in 1926, following a conference in Locarno, Switzerland, at which the French diplomat Aristide Briand made a famous speech, saying, "Away with rifles, machine guns, and cannon! Make way for conciliation, arbitration, and peace!" Once Germany had entered, however, its delegate began complaining bitterly about the organization's powerlessness and inefficiency. The chief German delegate, Gustav Stresemann, said, "If we [the principals in a particular dispute] had all been gathered at one table . . . we should have arranged everything in one afternoon. As it is, the Geneva people take weeks and settle nothing at all. . . . They promised the nations a paradise and they gave them torrents of paper."

Things rapidly went downhill for the league. After the Nazi party scored a smashing victory in

European leaders, including Italian dictator Benito Mussolini (left) meet in Locarno, Switzerland in 1925. The Locarno conference resulted in agreements designed to bring peace and stability to Europe and Germany's admittance to the League of Nations.

the 1930 German election, there was little the league could do to halt Germany's open aggression and rearmament. Two other actions—Japan's invasion of Manchuria in 1931 and Italy's seizure in 1935 of Ethiopia, in which both countries simply ignored league sanctions—showed how feeble the league's abilities were outside Europe as well. When Hitler joined with Japan's military leadership and Mussolini to form the Axis powers, the threat of war seemed inevitable.

By the mid-1930s most nations had abandoned all hope for the league as a peacekeeping force. Only those countries most threatened by invasion, such as Czechoslovakia, France, and the Soviet Union, asked other members to continue their pledge of joint security. The covenant had failed, and member nations had no reason to abide by it. When Germany finally invaded Poland in 1939, France and England declared war on the aggressor and World War II began.

Adolf Hitler speaks to Nazi party members and troops. The league could do little to stop Germany's open aggression and rearmament.

2

The Birth of the United Nations

I will say that he must indeed be a blind soul who cannot see that some great purpose and design is being worked out here below, of which we have the honor to be the faithful servants.
—Winston Churchill before the U.S. Congress, promoting the formation of the United Nations

LONG BEFORE WORLD War II even broke out, it was clear that a new organization—more powerful, more persuasive, and more respected than the League of Nations—was needed. That organization was the United Nations.

Its birth really began during World War II. The first clear milestone was a meeting at St. James' Palace in London in 1941 that brought together high-level representatives of all the Allied forces except the United States, which had not yet formally entered the war. These delegates signed a document, the Inter-Allied Declaration, pledging that they would "work together, and with other free peoples, both in war and in peace" toward worldwide social and economic security.

Although not yet formally at war, the United States was close to it—the Japanese attack on

(Opposite page) American soldiers during World War II tend to a wounded comrade in Okinawa, Japan. When the war ended, world leaders created the United Nations in hopes that the world would never again have to experience the horrors of war.

Pearl Harbor, after which America joined the battle, was to come in December of that year. But President Franklin D. Roosevelt and the British prime minister, Winston Churchill, were already in close contact over America's imminent entry. Roosevelt and Churchill, who had formed a close personal friendship as well as a strong professional bond, were especially interested in creating a new agency to oversee world peace. Roosevelt, wary of an isolationist reaction similar to that which Wilson had encountered, was determined to start the wheels turning even before the end of the war.

Two months after the signing of the Inter-Allied Declaration, Roosevelt and Churchill met on a warship off the coast of Newfoundland, Canada, to discuss and sign the Atlantic Charter. It pledged similar mutual support between the United States and England to that provided for in the Inter-Allied pact and promised "a peace which will afford all nations the means of dwelling safely within their own boundaries in freedom from fear and want."

U.S. president Franklin D. Roosevelt (left) and British prime minister Winston Churchill meet on a warship off the coast of Newfoundland, Canada. The discussion and signing of the Atlantic Charter raised hopes for peace.

Both the American and British leaders felt that the agreement was a preliminary but important step. Churchill, reporting to his cabinet, said, "We must regard this as an interim and partial statement of war aims, designed to assure all countries of our righteous purpose." And in a radio broadcast after the signing was announced, American diplomat Clark Eichelberger said:

> Somehow, millions of people in the world tonight, hearing of the Roosevelt-Churchill Conference, feel that they have been snatched from the brink of disaster and their feet put upon the road to victory and world organization. It will be a long road, entailing many hardships—even, as Mr. Churchill predicted for his country, blood, sweat, toil, and tears. But it is the only road that will lead to victory and permanent peace. It is the road that the American people, with other brave nations, must travel.

An organization is born

Churchill was a guest at the White House the Christmas following Pearl Harbor, promoting what he called the Grand Alliance, a united force, to include America, against the Axis powers. His mission was a success. On New Year's Day 1942 all the new Allies—including the United States—signed a pledge of mutual support, the Declaration of United Nations. It said, in part, that the twenty-six signers were "convinced that complete victory over their enemies is essential to defend life, liberty, independence and religious freedom, and to preserve human rights and justice in their own lands as well as other lands."

Besides America and the United Kingdom those countries signing the declaration were: Australia, Belgium, Canada, China, Costa Rica, Cuba, Czechoslovakia, the Dominican Republic, El Salvador, Greece, Guatemala, Haiti, Honduras, India, Luxembourg, the Netherlands, New Zealand, Nicaragua, Norway, Panama, Poland, the Soviet

Union, the Union of South Africa, and Yugoslavia. France and Denmark, which had been associated with the Allies since the beginning, were at the time occupied by Nazi forces; after their liberation they also became formal signers.

The occasion marked the first formal use of a phrase suggested by Roosevelt: the United Nations. According to legend Roosevelt awakened one morning with the phrase in his head. He got into his wheelchair (he had been disabled by polio as a young man), wheeled himself across the hall to the suite where Churchill was staying, and called out, "How about 'the United Nations'?" Churchill was taking a bath at the time. After a few long moments of consideration, the British prime minister replied, "That should do it."

Dumbarton Oaks and Yalta

Another major milestone came in the fall of 1944, when the Allied nations held a series of meetings at Dumbarton Oaks, a mansion in Washington, D.C. The Dumbarton Oaks Conference laid out the basic structure and guidelines for the future United Nations Organization, including the basic three-part structure of the General Assembly, the Security Council, and the Secretariat.

U.S. secretary of state Cordell Hull (third from left) opens the second phase of talks at Dumbarton Oaks. The basic structure and guidelines for the future UN were laid out at this conference.

Churchill (left), Roosevelt (center), and Soviet leader Joseph Stalin (right) meet at Yalta. By the time of the Yalta meeting it was clear that the Allies were winning the war.

Further details were worked out as the war continued. By the time Roosevelt, Churchill, and Soviet leader Joseph Stalin met in February 1945 at Yalta, on the Crimean Peninsula, it was clear that the Allies were winning the war. A convention at San Francisco was planned for later that year, when the new organization's charter would be formally written.

Writing the charter

The San Francisco Conference convened in April 1945 at a crucial moment in history—only a few weeks after Roosevelt's death, less than a month short of Germany's surrender, and four months before Japan's surrender.

The countries invited were those that had declared war on Germany or Japan as of March 1, 1945, and who had signed the Declaration of United Nations. Delegates from these countries—fifty-one altogether—were given the responsibility of creating a charter for the new United Nations, based on the guidelines set down at Dumbarton Oaks. As at the openings of both the Con-

Delegates of fifty-one nations meet in San Francisco to create a charter for the UN. Despite high hopes, the first days of the conference were beset by tension and conflict.

gress of Vienna and the League of Nations, hopes ran high. Gen. Carlos Peña Romulo of the Philippines, in one of the convention's opening speeches, declared, "Let us make this floor the last battlefield."

In some ways the conference itself turned into a battlefield. The whole world was still reeling from the war, and the conflict between the so-called Free World and the Eastern block, or communist bloc, led by the Soviet Union, had escalated dramatically. This tension led to the conference's first controversy, which came only hours after the opening speeches. It is customary in international conferences to have the host country's representative lead the sessions. But Vyacheslav Mikhailovich Molotov, the head of the Soviet delegation, vigorously objected to the U.S. delegate, Secretary of State Edward Stettinius, running the conference by himself.

A compromise was eventually reached, in which the United States presided over the steering and executive committees, with rotating chairs for the plenary (full) sessions. The Soviet-U.S. conflict set the combative tone for the conference and, indeed, for the UN in years to come. This "instant display of fierce partisanship [allegiance] in small matters," as historian Cornelia Meigs described it, was an abrupt and unwelcome beginning to a conference devoted to international cooperation.

Finding a structure

Despite this rocky start, the conference proceeded. The delegates formalized the basic structure for the organization: a General Assembly that would include delegates from all the member nations, a smaller Security Council made up of both permanent and rotating members, and a Secretariat that would be responsible for the organization's day-to-day, internal administration. Conference participants also formalized the concept of veto power, or the ability of one nation to reject action proposed by others. This power, given only to permanent members of the Security Council, would play a crucial role later.

The work of writing the charter was enormous in scope and difficulty, with countless needs to be met and endless crises to be confronted. There were broad philosophical questions to wrestle with, including the organization's basic purpose, its role in world politics and economics, and its ability to serve as a means of diplomacy rather than coercion, or domination by force.

There were also practical problems, large and small. The growing tension between the United States and the Soviet Union needed delicate handling. The UN's International Court of Justice, a direct successor to the League of Nations' World Court, had to be organized, as did organizations devoted to such specialized areas as famine relief and refugees. The design of the organization's official flag had to be chosen, and its official languages agreed upon.

The first sessions

The final language of the charter reflected a determination to uphold the four basic principles agreed on by all: "to save succeeding generations from the scourge of war," "to reaffirm faith in fundamental human rights," "to establish conditions under which . . . international law can be maintained," and "to promote social progress." Its eloquent preamble was written by a committee headed by Field Marshal Jan Smuts, who had done so much to create the League of Nations and became prime minister of the Union of South Africa in 1939. Though watered down in its final form, the preamble reflected Smuts's hope that it be "in language which should appeal to the hearts as well as the minds of men."

The International Court of Justice (pictured) was one of many specialized agencies established in the UN's earliest days.

U.S. president Harry S Truman delivers the closing address at the last session of the San Francisco Conference, three days after the delegates had unanimously adopted the final UN charter.

On June 25, 1945—only two months after the conference began—the delegates met at the San Francisco Opera House and unanimously adopted a final charter. It was signed the next day in a ceremony at the Veterans Memorial Hall. Wellington Koo of China, representing the first country attacked by the Axis powers, was the first to sign. Harry S Truman, who had succeeded Roosevelt as U.S. president, lifted his arms high at the ceremony and exclaimed, "Oh! What a great day this can be in history!" At the same ceremony, Lord Halifax of England said, "Let us, alike mindful of the world's need and our own weakness, pray that under God's guidance what we have done here in the last weeks will be found worthy of the faith which gave it birth, and of the human suffering which has been its price."

The charter officially took effect in October of that year, and the first sessions of the General As-

British prime minister Clement Attlee addresses delegates during the first session of the UN General Assembly.

sembly and Security Council were held early in 1946. The meetings took place in temporary, humble quarters in London, a city still in chaos after being severely bombed by the Germans. In his opening statements to the General Assembly, Dr. Zuleta Angel, the Colombian representative, paid tribute to the wartime courage of London when he said, "We have come to the British capital, which bears upon it the deep [imprint] of heroic majesty."

Pressing tasks

The delegates at those first working meetings had their jobs cut out for them. The freedom of former European colonies, international labor relations, refugee issues, and international justice were all important and urgent concerns. But perhaps the most pressing task of all was to deal

with the issue of disarmament and the new, related question of nuclear power; it had been less
than half a year since America had ended the war
with Japan by atomic force.

The General Assembly moved quickly to create the Atomic Energy Commission (later re-
named International Atomic Energy Agency), the
International Court of Justice, and the International Refugee Organization. It also dealt with
smaller, more specific issues. The first complaint
requiring attention from the new Security Council, for example, came from Iran. Iran sought the
council's help with the Soviet Union, which had
not withdrawn its wartime troops from the north-
ern Iranian province of Azerbaijan.

The second half of the first session was held in
New York City in October 1946. The delegates
completed the Universal Declaration of Human
Rights, which formed the basis for the UN's
stand on human rights. It also made formal con-
nections with such existing groups as the International Labor Organization and the Food and Agriculture Organization. Despite this activity the UN
was already beginning to hear criticisms that it
was as ineffective and protocol-bound as the
League of Nations. To these charges, General Assembly president Paul-Henri Spaak of Belgium
replied: "There are people who doubt, who make
jokes, and who, basing their whole attitude on all
that is difficult, complicated, and necessarily im-
perfect in our work, are ready to announce our
failure. They are wrong today."

The search for a permanent home

The question of where to headquarter the UN
illustrates the delicate political problems the delegates faced in running the new group. Many
countries offered to host it, and several possibilities were seriously considered—chiefly Geneva,

the home of the League of Nations, and London, where the UN's early meetings had taken place.

But the Soviet Union, still recovering from the devastations of war and formulating its own plans for Europe, was eager to choose a spot in a non-European setting. America seemed a logical choice, and in December 1945 Congress voted unanimously to invite the UN to make its permanent home there. Unlike Wilson, Roosevelt had succeeded in maintaining American enthusiasm about involvement in a world government organization. The American offer was accepted, and New York City was the favored site.

The first temporary quarters were established at Hunter College in the Bronx, a borough of New York City. The mood was generally optimistic and informal, with the makeshift lodgings creating a convivial atmosphere. One unexpected voice during this period symbolized the early high hopes that the world had for the UN. As teams of carpenters worked feverishly to remodel

Former First Lady Eleanor Roosevelt holds a copy of the Universal Declaration of Human Rights, which formed the basis for the UN's stand on human rights.

the facilities at Hunter, a ballot box was installed. When the box was opened, before any voting began, this note was found:

> May I, who have had the privilege of fabricating this ballot box, cast the first vote? May God be with every member of the United Nations Organization and through your noble efforts bring lasting peace to us all. All over the world.
> —Paul Antonio, Mechanic

Life at Hunter finally proved too frustrating, however. For one thing, there was not enough room at the college itself, and delegates were often forced to meet in cramped conference centers and hotel rooms around the city. Considerable time was wasted simply in negotiating traffic from one meeting to the next. The next base of operations was a former Sperry Gyroscope factory on Long Island, but that proved no more satisfactory.

New York City

Finally, in late 1946, a permanent home was found in the Turtle Bay neighborhood of New York City. Turtle Bay is a neighborhood on Manhattan's East Side, between 42nd and 48th streets and bordering the East River. Before 1946 it was primarily an area of low-income tenements, slaughterhouses, and breweries. Millionaire John D. Rockefeller Jr., at the request of his son Nelson, bought an eighteen-acre parcel of land there from a developer and donated it to the UN. The Rockefeller family had been strong supporters of the League of Nations—among their gifts had been money to build its library—and they were willing to support the new organization as well.

The city of New York immediately offered land adjacent to the site, along with waterfront rights and a promise of neighborhood reconstruction. The federal government provided an interest-free loan to aid in construction. An international committee of designers, architects, and consultants drew up plans for the new buildings: the thirty-nine story Secretariat Building, the long, low Conference Building, and the General Assembly Hall. (The Dag Hammarskjöld Library was added later.)

The cornerstone was laid on October 24, 1949—the anniversary of the day the charter took effect, now celebrated every year as United Nations Day. Construction moved quickly after that; portions were occupied as early as the summer of 1950, and the General Assembly held its first meeting in its new hall in October 1952.

Symbols of peace

The new buildings reflected the diverse cultures of the UN's member nations. The Security Council chamber was designed by a Norwegian. The bronze doors of the General Assembly building were a gift from Canada. A committee room was panelled in British oak. The Netherlands presented

Millionaire John D. Rockefeller, a strong supporter of the League of Nations, donated an eighteen-acre parcel of land in New York to the UN. This land, along with adjacent land donated by the U.S. government, became the UN's new home.

a golden sphere and pendulum that record the rotation of the earth. Statues made of satinwood, symbolizing peace and prosperity, were gifts of Indonesia. A peace bell came from Japan. A model of Sputnik, the world's first artificial satellite, came from the Soviet Union. American schoolchildren collected fifty thousand dollars to finance a fountain outside the Secretariat. All in all, it became a truly international building complex.

On October 24, 1949, UN officials place historical documents into a steel box to be laid inside the cornerstone at the new UN headquarters in New York.

3

The United Nations as Peacekeeper

*We the people of the United Nations, deter-
mined to save succeeding generations from the
scourge of war, which twice in our lifetime has
brought untold sorrow to mankind. . . .*
—from the preamble to the UN Charter

THE UNITED NATIONS has historically had one primary job, important above all others: to keep the peace. In the past this has required two major functions: solving immediate disputes and working on long-range problems such as disarmament and nuclear control.

The UN has generally done this through such passive actions as sending unarmed observer missions to gather information, dispatching treaty negotiators, and maintaining cease-fire agreements. Since the early 1990s, however, the UN has taken on a more active role. It has shifted its focus in some areas from peacekeeping to peacemaking. As it has become more willing and able to perform the more rigorous duties of peacemaking, important issues have arisen involving the formation of a permanent, proactive UN military force.

*(Opposite page) The UN flag is
raised in Cambodia, as UN
troops from Japan arrive to take
part in peacekeeping efforts.
Peacekeeping has remained the
primary job of the UN since its
inception.*

47

The primary body that acts on peace and security issues is the Security Council. It is made up of five permanent members and ten rotating members. The permanent members initially represented the victors in World War II, known as the Big Five: the United States, the Soviet Union, the United Kingdom, France, and Nationalist China, also known as Taiwan. The People's Republic of China has since replaced Taiwan on the Security Council. In addition to the five permanent Security Council members, ten nonpermanent seats are elected by the General Assembly and held in rotation, normally for two years.

Solving disputes

At one point in the UN's planning stages, Franklin D. Roosevelt had a notion that the Security Council should hold its meetings on a remote island, far from the world's trouble spots. It was also suggested early on that just the opposite occur—that the Security Council meet in troubled locations such as Jerusalem or Berlin to underline the UN's determination to attack world crises and conflicts head on. In the end, however, the coun-

Members of the UN Security Council meet in 1947. The Security Council tries to provide guidance for resolving disputes between nations.

UN soldiers from Chile stand at attention to honor a visiting official in Cambodia. UN troops dress in the uniforms of their countries but wear blue helmets or blue berets to distinguish themselves as UN peacekeepers.

cil's headquarters were established in New York, at the main UN headquarters.

Any nation in the world, UN member or not, can bring a matter before the Security Council for guidance in solving a dispute. No matter how large or how small a country is, the Council will listen to its complaint. Henry Cabot Lodge, the U.S. delegate to the UN in 1954, summed up this philosophy when he responded to a request for observers from Thailand, which was experiencing unrest following a political coup d'état: "I hope I will never live to see the day when a small country comes to the UN to ask for protection against war, and is simply greeted with the question, 'What's the hurry?'"

If disputing countries cannot find a peaceful solution on their own, the council suggests terms of agreement. If the problem still remains, the council can impose economic and diplomatic sanctions against an offender. If necessary it can then authorize military actions by volunteer troops from member states. These troops dress in the uniforms of their countries but wear blue helmets or blue berets to show their status as UN

Many harsh words have been spoken and much vigorous debate conducted in the conference room of the UN Security Council.

peacekeepers, and they are armed with light defensive weapons.

The power of the veto

The actions of these troops historically have been limited to passive observation and treaty negotiations. One reason for this limitation was the so-called veto rule. When the Security Council was formed, it was felt that cooperation among the most powerful countries was absolutely necessary. In the words of U.S. secretary of state Cordell Hull, "Unless the Great Powers agree, we cannot hope to have peace."

The UN's organizers agreed to allow any permanent member to veto an action, even if the other four were in agreement. In other words, if there was not complete cooperation, or unanimity, among the Big Five, no action could be taken. (This policy is in contrast to that of the General Assembly, where every state's vote has equal weight.)

Sometimes the Security Council's style of decision making worked well, but often problems arose when the power was abused. Such was the case with the Soviet Union, which often disagreed with the other council members and did not hesitate to use its veto power extensively. (The other permanent members used the veto sparingly; the United States and China, for instance, have used it only one time each.)

The Soviet veto effectively paralyzed the council for decades, preventing it from taking a more vigorous role than passive observation. In 1950, frustrated by the deadlock, the General Assembly passed a resolution, the Uniting for Peace Resolution, that gave the assembly authority to act on a threat to peace if the Security Council, "because of lack of unanimity of the permanent members, fails to exercise its primary responsibility." This has helped the UN negotiate around council deadlocks on a number of occasions.

Treaties and cease-fires

For most of its history, the UN's military actions have been modest. Rather than actively taking sides in a dispute, UN troops have simply tried to stop bloodshed. American diplomat Clark Eichelberger has said that a UN peacekeeping mission "has no enemy. It is an impartial body, not there to secure a victory for one side or another."

Often the mere presence of a UN force has been enough to avoid violent conflict and prompt rational discussion. One example is the Cuban missile crisis of 1962. In response to the presence of Soviet missiles in Cuba, U.S. president John F. Kennedy launched a naval blockade against Cuba and asked the Security Council to intervene. This confrontation between the superpowers could easily have escalated into nuclear war. So the world waited anxiously to see how it would be resolved. Thanks to the diplomacy of Secretary General U Thant and others, however, the UN succeeded in halting Soviet arms shipments to Cuba.

The United States called off the blockade, and

Cuban dictator Fidel Castro (left) shakes hands with Secretary-General U Thant. The diplomacy of Thant and others aided UN success in halting Soviet arms shipments to Cuba.

negotiations between the superpowers began. Concerning the UN's role during the crisis, Eichelberger noted:

> Let us picture the U.S. and the Soviet Union deadlocked in the Caribbean, without a Security Council where they could appear and where the hopes of all mankind could be expressed. It is hard to see how one or the other could have pulled back from such a perilous position. Indeed, one could say that if there had been no UN the two giants might have confronted each other with disaster.

Not all UN peacekeeping actions have been as successful. Since 1974 UN forces have maintained a shaky cease-fire on the island of Cyprus between the Greek majority and Turkish minority populations. Greek and Turkish Cypriots alike have threatened violent takeovers both before and since the UN's intervention. It is widely believed that the organization's presence there has done little to resolve the longstanding ethnic dispute.

Critics contend that, as long as such temporary cease-fires exist, there is little pressure on either side to negotiate a real peace. These makeshift agreements can drag on for years with little change. As Greek Cypriot president Georgios Vassilou has said, "The duty of the world is not ended by setting up the peace-keeping forces. Peacekeeping is not peacemaking. The only reason for peacekeeping is to stop the killing and give time for peacemaking."

Changing times

Many observers feel that the waning of the cold war has dramatically changed the UN's potential to make and keep the peace. This is borne out by the recent record of UN peacekeeping missions. In its first forty-three years the UN undertook only thirteen such missions. In just six recent years, however—from 1986 to 1992—it has undertaken another thirteen.

A Swedish member of the UN peacekeeping force in Cyprus. The UN has maintained a shaky cease-fire between the Greek and Turkish communities on the island since 1974.

The UN has about a dozen ongoing, large-scale peacekeeping operations around the world. A few, such as those in the Middle East, have been continuous since the organization's start. Fully half of them, however, did not begin until after the breakup of the Soviet Union.

These newer missions are far more ambitious than the simple patrolling of cease-fire lines. Recent duties have included disarming warring factions (as in El Salvador) and functioning essentially as substitute governments in the absence of stable law and order (as in Cambodia).

Some of these missions have not succeeded in achieving their goals. UN-backed economic sanctions and resolutions against Iraq, for instance, failed to stop that country's aggression against Kuwait and led to the UN-sanctioned Persian Gulf War. In Angola a UN-sponsored peace accord failed because it tried to achieve its goals

UN troops disembark from helicopters at Battambang airport in Cambodia, where they act as a substitute government in the absence of stable law and order.

too quickly; because the UN failed to fully disarm both sides in the long civil war there before elections were organized, fighting resumed soon after the election.

One of the largest of the current peacekeeping operations is in Cambodia. As of late 1992 the UN had over twenty thousand soldiers, police, and civilians there as part of a $2-billion-a-year operation designed to enable elections, stabilize the economy and government, and prevent warfare between the Khmer Rouge guerrilla faction and the ruling Phnom Penh government. Few details have been ignored in this operation. The UN presence even extends into the voting hut, where Polaroid cameras have been installed to guard against voter fraud.

This ambitious project has cast the UN in the role of functioning as a substitute government in Cambodia. This is a vast undertaking for an organization that has previously been cautious about intervening in a country's internal affairs, and the UN is still searching for its proper role there. In effect, the UN has nearly turned Cambodia into a protectorate—that is, an area directly under the supervision of another country or agency. Yasushi Akashi, the UN diplomat in charge of the organization's activities there, has said, "I don't appreciate the term 'protectorate,' but I do not know how else to describe this unprecedented situation."

Grand ideals

Playing the role of peacekeeper is rarely easy. While most countries support the idea of a world body that can help resolve disputes and keep the peace, many of these same countries bristle at the thought of UN intervention in their own affairs. What may to one country be legitimate intervention in a violent dispute can to another be simple (and unwanted) meddling. The UN constantly travels between these two points seeking a middle ground in its efforts to make and keep the peace.

Some of the problems hampering UN peace-keeping efforts are self-inflicted. Under UN policy, for example, peacekeeping troops carry only light arms and are permitted to fire only in self-defense. They are not equipped to wage war, nor are they allowed to. Even in a war zone, where violence is a constant threat, UN peacekeeping troops must show restraint. Their job is to keep the peace, not add to the conflict. Rules such as this sometimes endanger peacekeeping troops as well as those they are assigned to protect. In January 1993, for example, heavily armed Serbian gunmen shot to death a Bosnian government official who was traveling with a UN convoy. His UN escorts could do little to stop the attack. This and other instances of passive UN responses to

violent situations serve as examples in the ongoing effort to strengthen the organization's ability to act decisively.

Critics charge that on a larger scale the UN's leadership has often been reluctant to take responsibility for serious peacekeeping efforts. They feel, for instance, that the UN's members—particularly the powerful Security Council's Big Five—make fine speeches about upholding the grand ideals of peace then refuse to provide the financial means for real performance. Unless words are backed with action and resources, critics say, those words are useless. As journalist William Safire has noted, "Without the credible threat of a heavy stick, the carrots of diplomacy will have no takers."

Pitfalls

Critics—including the UN's own Secretary-General, Boutros Boutros-Ghali—also charge that the UN is so bogged down with bureaucratic red tape that quick action is impossible and that its various agencies are often overly reluctant to

UN Secretary-General Boutros Boutros-Ghali, among others, believes that excessive bureaucratic red tape prevents the UN from acting quickly and decisively.

make strong decisions. The organization has also been criticized for having a lack of foresight and clear, long-term analysis that would let it deal with growing problems before they become major disasters.

The turmoil that has befallen Somalia demonstrates some of the pitfalls that can arise from a lack of foresight, prompt response, and decisive action. Somalia's current chaos was created by a combination of factors, including drought, starvation, the toppling of ruler Mohammed Siad Barre, and subsequent clan warfare (between factions heavily armed with weapons obtained from both the United States and the Soviet Union). The country's government, military, law, and virtually

Somali refugees, fleeing civil war and famine, wait for food at a U.S. relief distribution point. The UN's slow response to the crisis in Somalia has been cited as an example of the organization's failings.

Pakistani members of the UN peacekeeping force man heavy machine guns as they patrol the airport area of Mogadishu, Somalia. The UN effort was seen as too little, too late.

all other social frameworks have disintegrated, leaving it in a state of complete disaster and near ruin.

The UN took a long time to react to the collapse of Somalia. When it finally sent troops to ensure that food and medical supplies would not be stolen by armed clans before they reached their destinations, the help was too little, too late. The UN was forced to ask American troops to intervene in late 1992; the subsequent action, Operation Restore Hope, succeeded in getting food to starving Somalis and, to a large degree, in stemming the violence.

In April and May 1993 U.S. troops were replaced with a UN force. Gen. Colin Powell, chairman of the U.S. Joint Chiefs of Staff, feels that the reins should be quickly handed over to avoid a protracted U.S. involvement: "It's sort of like the cavalry coming to the rescue, straightening things out for a while, and then letting the marshals come back in to keep things under control." However, some observers feel that if UN troops remain underarmed, outnumbered, and able to fire only in self-defense, they will not be able to prevent bloodshed.

Risks

One reason for the UN's reluctance to bring force to bear in Somalia has been a fear of becoming involved in a long, drawn-out affair requiring vast amounts of money, resources, and human energy. David Smock, a senior program officer at the United Nations Institute of Peace, has said, "If the UN force gets sucked into a morass [in Somalia], the international community will think twice before it commits itself again. If the operation is a marvelous success, that will also have an impact on future action."

UN officials also fear that if force is used to secure a chaotic situation, the risk of compromising future humanitarian aid is great. The UN's reputation rests on its being an impartial, neutral agency that favors no one except those in need, and if it uses force that reputation could change. As Sadako Ogata, the UN high commissioner for refugees, stated recently, "If forces are going to fight their way into a place, humanitarian organizations are going to have a very hard time following because their credibility as impartial organizations would be undermined."

4

The Environment, Health, and Social Development

A porous ozone shield could pose a greater threat to an exposed population than a hostile army. Drought and disease can decimate no less mercilessly than the weapons of war.
—Boutros Boutros-Ghali,
An Agenda for Peace

THE UNITED NATIONS' main goal has always been to promote world peace. But the UN has another function, one that is closely related to the first: to improve the daily life of the world's population through environmental, social, and economic programs.

The problems of food and famine, shelter, population control, economic development, drug abuse, health care, and the special problems of the environment, children, women, and the elderly, are closely connected to the problems of peacekeeping. By addressing them, the UN can attack the roots that often lie at the base of armed conflict.

The UN acts as a central clearinghouse for many specialized organizations in the fields of

(Opposite page) A Somali woman cradles her baby at a refugee camp in northeastern Kenya. In addition to promoting world peace the UN is committed to assisting the world's needy people.

61

A refugee feeds her children with food provided by CARE. Private organizations such as CARE assist the UN in the difficult mission of providing food and shelter to those in need.

social, environmental, and economic aid. A good number of these trace their origins to the original San Francisco conference, where participants vowed to pay special attention to social issues, economic development, and international cooperation and understanding.

This last goal has been a cornerstone of the UN's humanitarian efforts. In late 1945 at an early meeting of the UN Educational, Scientific, and Cultural Organization (UNESCO), the British prime minister, Clement Attlee, set the tone for the future when he said:

> Today the peoples of the world are islands shouting at each other over seas of misunderstanding. . . . "Know thyself," said the old proverb. "Know your neighbor," we say today. And the whole world is our neighbor.

UN organizations today perform such vital functions as delivering food and clothing to needy families, immunizing children against disease, coordinating disaster relief, sponsoring agricultural self-sufficiency, promoting trade and industrial development, and providing shelter for refugees. The UN does this with help from thousands of regional and governmental agencies, as well as such private organizations as the International Red Cross and CARE. Together, they form a network of assistance programs around the world.

The overall picture

Since Attlee made his remarks in 1945, the overall picture has brightened in some respects, such as in health care. The global balance sheet of human welfare remains grim, however. Annual income in the forty-one poorest countries is well below $300, compared to about $14,500 for developed countries. Seventy percent of the world's income is produced and consumed by fifteen percent of the population. Living standards in Latin America are lower today than in the 1970s, and African living standards have slipped to the level of the 1960s. Over 900 million adults worldwide are illiterate.

These problems have widened divisions between the affluent industrialized countries and the poorer developing countries. Thérese P. Sévigny,

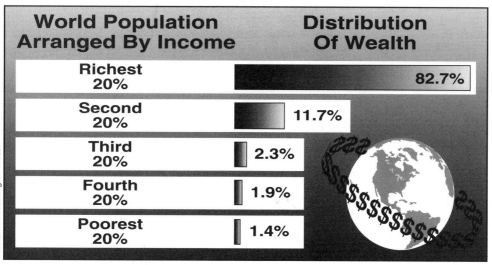

Source: *The Washington Times.*

Nigerian refugee children, suffering from malnutrition, are given a medical checkup at the French Army Field Hospital in Gabon in 1969. Millions of people in developing countries still live in absolute poverty.

undersecretary-general for public information, has written that in the last twenty years "the gap in living standards between the world's rich and poor has steadily grown. Industrialized countries and some parts of the developing world have prospered, but a billion people [still] live in absolute poverty."

The UN has addressed this situation by creating programs to answer every need. Many of these have been successful in stemming the tide of poverty, disease, and environmental degradation. But such a large network of agencies can also be tangled, and critics charge that waste and redundancy are commonplace. Journalist Shirley Hazzard recently wrote that "the confused state of the numerous UN relief agencies has been the subject of scandal and concern for many years."

Secretary-General Boutros-Ghali himself has strongly criticized the UN bureaucracy in the past. By allowing overlapping duties among agencies to interfere with their operations, he charges, the resulting aid is less effective. He recently introduced a plan for improving overall efficiency. This plan calls for eliminating excess personnel, merging similar agencies, cooperating more closely with groups such as Amnesty International, and making better use of UN agencies, such as the International Court of Justice.

The environment

One of the most crucial questions faced by UN agencies concerns the demands placed on the earth's resources as the world's population increases and more countries become industrialized. The problem of environmental degradation has become increasingly severe in recent years. James G. Speth of the World Resources Institute has said, "For the first time, human numbers and impacts have grown so large [that] they are eroding on a global scale the natural system that supports life."

Pollution of the sea and air, an increase in the greenhouse effect, hazardous waste management, and enormous energy requirements are just a few of the problems caused by industries in developed countries. Meanwhile, in developing countries, there is a rush to build factories or deforest huge tracts of trees for fuel. In both cases there are often few ways in which development's impact on the environment can be curbed.

Addressing the problems

The UN addresses these problems in a number of ways. One focus of UN-related environmental agencies is to monitor pollution caused by industrialized nations. For instance, the UN Environment Program, based in Nairobi, Kenya, helped develop a resource called the International Information System on the Environment (INFOTERRA), which is also based in Kenya. INFOTERRA links agencies that monitor aspects of the environment so that they can quickly share information and concerns.

Another focus is to encourage wise resource management and environmental education within developing countries. Helping poorer countries develop in an ecologically sensible way, many argue, is in everyone's best interests, because problems caused by environmental abuse create a ripple effect that is felt far beyond the problems' places of origin. As Mahbubul Haq, an environmental advisor to the UN, notes, "Poor people can be stopped at borders, but poverty can't be stopped. Poverty travels in the form of drugs, terrorism, global warming and AIDS."

The UN has also been a major organizer and participant in global environmental conferences, such as the 1992 Earth Summit in Rio de Janeiro, Brazil. The major concrete product of that confer-

A man carries one of the few remaining logs in a deforested section of the Amazon rain forest. The UN is working to prevent further damage to the environment.

UNITED NATIONS CONFERENCE ON
ENVIRONMENT AND DEVELOPMENT
Rio de Janeiro 3–14 June 1992

During the 1992 Earth Summit in Rio de Janeiro, Brazil, world leaders signed an international pact designed to curb global warming.

ence was the signing of an international pact designed to curb global warming.

Some of the UN's efforts have gone very slowly, however, and often mere talk takes the place of action. For instance a major law, called the UN Convention on the Law of the Sea, was drawn up over a decade ago; it would provide, for the first time, a comprehensive legal framework for institutions that manage and preserve the marine environment. But the law remains unsigned by a majority of UN members while they debate specific points within it. Meanwhile, the sea is becoming increasingly more polluted and entire species of animals are in danger of extinction.

The major challenge in the UN's environmental actions lies in balancing economic growth and development with the preservation of an increasingly fragile ecosystem. The world cannot survive without a sensible harmony between development and preservation. As Gro Harlem Brundtland, then the prime minister of Norway, wrote in the introduction to a major 1972 UN report on the environment: "The environment is where we all live; development is what we all do in attempting to improve our lot within that abode. The two are inseparable."

Another major humanitarian problem addressed by the UN is that of supplying enough food to feed everyone on the planet. The problem encompasses not only short-term emergency aid for the victims of famine or natural disasters, but also long-term development of sensible agricultural programs to ensure that food can be reliably grown and distributed year after year.

Food and agriculture

Short-term emergency aid for the victims of famine or natural disasters is primarily handled by the UN Disaster Relief Organization (UNDRO). The Food and Agriculture Organization (FAO), meanwhile, is concerned with supplying food and training to developing countries over the long term.

FAO coordinates international programs to provide donated food to needy countries or store it for emergencies. In 1987, for instance, FAO's World Food Program shipped a record amount: $1.1 billion from one hundred countries in cash and commodities. These supplies went to seventy-nine operations in thirty-two countries, affecting some fifteen million people. In addition, seven hundred thousand tons of food were given to the International Emergency Food Reserve.

FAO also provides, to local agencies, educational programs and materials on such topics as soil conservation, animal care, farming techniques, and wise energy use. These projects include agriculture, fisheries, forestry, livestock, and land reform.

The challenges of providing long- and short-term food aid point up the problems of a large, political bureaucracy like the UN. UNDRO and FAO have often been criticized for their relative slowness in acting. For instance, the UN was ac-

A gannet, a bird known for its striking white plumage, lies dead on a beach, a victim of oil pollution. The UN is attempting to combat the ocean pollution that threatens some animal species.

cused of ignoring for years before it became critical the worsening famine in Somalia. UN inaction left the country without clear distribution lines for emergency food supplies, the primary reason that American forces intervened.

Some critics say that the UN could benefit from the lessons learned in Somalia. Speed, decisiveness, and flexibility are lacking, they say, from the makeup of UN relief organizations. Journalist Ray Bonner recently suggested that a corps of dedicated volunteers would be better suited to the task, rather than career civil servants who might be too timid to intervene. He wrote, "It wasn't only that UN officials refused to take any initiative [in Somalia]. Far worse, they even declined to act when asked. . . . If, in the future, the UN hopes to avoid failures like [that] in Somalia, it will need to change on a more fundamental level."

Health

The health situation in the world today is another critical area of concern for the UN. Each year, there are some 250 thousand polio cases and 3 million deaths due to measles, tetanus, or pertussis. Nearly half of the world's population still

Workers unload bags of wheat flour in Maseru, Lesotho, in southern Africa. UN relief efforts usually involve assistance from many nations and other relief organizations.

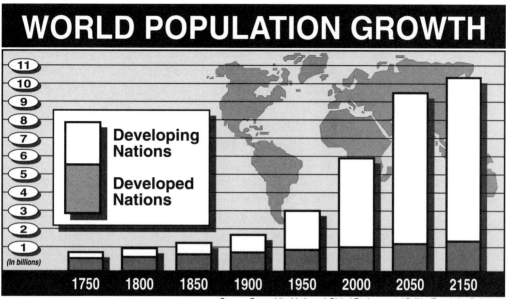

WORLD POPULATION GROWTH

11
10
9
8
7
6
5
4
3
2
1
(In billions)

Developing Nations

Developed Nations

1750 1800 1850 1900 1950 2000 2050 2150

Source: *Beyond the Limits* and *Global Environmental Politics/Population Bulletin 42.*

lives in areas where the risk of malaria is extremely high. Diseases such as AIDS, tuberculosis, cancer, and cardiovascular disease continue to be major killers.

Global population, meanwhile, has topped 5 billion and is increasing at a rate of 220 thousand a day. It will reach 6 billion by the end of the century. The largest population increases are occurring in developing countries, where 9 out of 10 new births take place. These young children are particularly vulnerable to disease because many of these countries are unable to provide proper care for the new population. Every day, 40 thousand children die of preventable disease or starvation—a total of 14 million every year.

The UN's chief agency for health is the World Health Organization (WHO), headquartered in Geneva, Switzerland. It provides information and assistance to physical, mental, and environmental health agencies worldwide. But perhaps its most important work is in providing such basic health care services as immunization. An estimated one million people in developing countries are reached every year by WHO programs.

UNICEF, the United Nations Children's Fund, addresses the special needs of children by providing long-term programs, such as day-care centers, as well as direct shipments of medical and school supplies. UNICEF reaches more than a billion children through age fifteen in 199 countries every year. One of its primary goals is to vaccinate 75 percent of the world's children against deadly diseases by 1995.

Such projects also serve a secondary purpose: teaching local communities about the relationship between a nation's future and the health of its citizens. Singer Harry Belafonte, a goodwill ambassador for UNICEF, has said, "When UNICEF . . . puts an immunization program in a place, many of these countries begin to understand that immunization is so fundamental to the future of society, and that it is perhaps the greatest investment they can make. It is also the cheapest."

What we owe each other

The agencies mentioned here are just a few of the UN-related organizations that form its vast and complex resource network. All are working for a single purpose: harmony between an improved human condition and a preserved environment.

The health of the world and the world's inhabitants, generally speaking, have both radically improved and rapidly deteriorated in the years since the UN began addressing these problems. Much of the improvement in areas such as disease control can be credited to the UN. However, the overall situation remains critical.

National cuts in welfare budgets, especially in Africa, are threatening to cause an overall drop in health services worldwide. The increase in world environmental problems aggravates health prob-

A Nicaraguan woman grimaces as she receives an immunization shot, provided by the World Health Organization (WHO). WHO annually immunizes about one million people in developing countries.

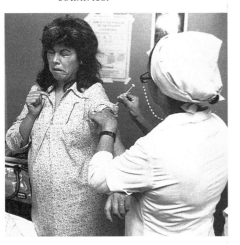

lems; for instance, a situation such as massive deforestation fosters the spread of disease by creating poor sanitation and water. And, despite efforts at stemming the population explosion, more and more people are taxing limited health resources. The challenge for the future will be to maintain and expand the fight against disease and overpopulation while maintaining a clean environment.

The men and women within the UN network of agencies recognize that helping others will ultimately benefit us all. As former U.S. ambassador to the UN Adlai Stevenson once stated in an address to the General Assembly about aid to starving countries: "It is necessary assistance, not charity. It is help we owe each other and owe ourselves."

For the sake of these school children in East Africa and children around the globe, the UN's greatest challenge may be bringing the world's countries together to improve life for all.

5

Human Rights
and Refugee Aid

---

*In serving [others], we recognize a simple but
powerful truth: we need each other.*
　　　　　　　　　—President Bill Clinton,
　　　　　　　　　inaugural address, January 1993

ALONG WITH A dedication to peace, security, and human welfare, the UN has always had a
strong commitment to watching out for other basic
rights of human beings. Its chief guiding light in
these matters is the Universal Declaration of Human Rights, which was prepared by the UN Commission on Human Rights shortly after the UN's
formation in 1946 and formally adopted in 1948.

The Universal Declaration of Human Rights

The declaration has its roots in a speech made
by Franklin D. Roosevelt. In this 1941 speech
Roosevelt spoke of Nazi human rights violations
and identified what he believed to be four basic
human freedoms: the freedom of expression,
freedom to worship, freedom from want, and
freedom from fear.

The commission's declaration reflects these
ideas. It encourages respect for "the highest aspi-
rations of the common people . . . faith in funda-

*(Opposite page) Amnesty
International members protest
human rights abuses in China,
where freedom of expression is
often not permitted. The UN's
Universal Declaration of
Human Rights supports freedom
of expression as a basic human
right.*

mental human rights, in the dignity and worth of the human person, in the equal rights of men and women and of nations large and small." It further guarantees "human rights and fundamental freedoms for all [people] without distinction as to race, sex, language or religion."

Specifically, the declaration affirms the right to equal protection against discrimination, arbitrary arrest or exile, slavery, cruel or inhuman punishment, equal opportunity under the law, a fair trial, the right to privacy, freedom of residence and movement within a home country, political asylum, freedom to marry without restriction of race, nationality, or religion, and the freedom to own property. Further articles affirm the universal right to freedom of thought, conscience, religion, opinion, speech, assembly, and participation in one's own government.

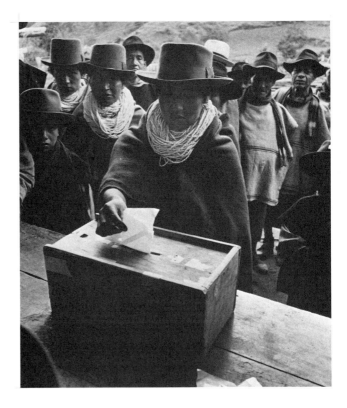

Indians in Guambia, Colombia, vote in an election for the governor of their district. The election, conducted by the government and five international organizations, including the UN, aims to improve living conditions in the region.

Over the years emphasis on specific violations has changed. Currently the UN's focus is on the topics of genocide, slavery and forced labor, the persecution of refugees, racial discrimination, discrimination against women, hostage taking, and torture. There is also concern for the rights of ethnic minorities, native or indigenous peoples, and migrant workers.

Demonstrators protest human rights abuses in Chile, where government forces have been accused of torturing thousands. Government-sponsored torture has long concerned UN officials.

Enforcement

The adoption of the declaration by the General Assembly was an important step in international responsibility for human rights—in fact, it was the largest single such step ever taken. However, enforcement of these human rights has not been simple.

Publishing a set of doctrines is one thing; enforcing it is another. It is easy for a government to preach freedom of the press, for example, while strictly regulating who gets to operate that press. The UN has consistently found it difficult

Returnees to El Salvador receive food aid as part of an assistance package provided by the UN. Following the cease-fire and UN-negotiated armistice, many former refugees returned to their country.

to make some of its member nations adhere strictly to its human rights code.

Part of the problem was the original declaration, which limited UN authority to making only studies and recommendations on human rights violations. A set of covenants that gave the UN concrete ways to take action against them was not ratified until 1976. Even when it can clearly identify human rights violations, the UN can do little more than bring them to public attention. Public attention can be beneficial in that a country may change its behavior to avoid further embarrassment. But this does not always occur.

Brutality in El Salvador

In 1993 the UN released a report accusing the government of El Salvador of brutally repressing criticism of the ruling military government. The report charged that the government had tortured and killed thousands of civilians suspected of opposing government policies. The government responded by pardoning hundreds of military officials and others who are thought to have carried out these actions.

This was not the response the UN had hoped for. But this event raises a point that human rights groups such as Amnesty International and Humanities Watch have tried to make over the years: that the UN acts too slowly and timidly to bring a quick end to human rights violations. El Salvador, a country called a "human rights disaster area" by Aryeh Neier, a longtime human rights observer who writes for *The Nation*, illustrates this point.

After twelve years of monitoring the fighting in El Salvador, the UN mission there finally succeeded in disarming warring factions, patching together a fragile cease-fire, and engineering a signed armistice. Not a single serious violation of the cease-fire was reported in the year leading up to the peace accord signings. But the UN has also been accused of passivity and of allowing largely cosmetic changes to take the place of real reform.

Critics charge that the UN's reluctance to act for fear of imposing on the sovereign rights of a nation has interfered with the rights of individuals inside that country. Recently Americas Watch, a private human rights organization, stated:

> The UN has avoided timely public criticism of the government on human rights matters, even when such criticism is warranted, and even when its own investigations have pointed to state involvement in abuses. [The UN] has opted for a conservative application of its mandate, one in which human rights problems are treated with the same kind of cautious diplomacy that one might use in attempting to resolve political disputes.

One method of persuasion that the UN can bring to bear on a country that is violating the human rights of its citizens is the imposition of economic and diplomatic sanctions. These are a form of boycott in which a country is forced by nonviolent persuasion to change its actions.

For many years the UN and other international groups, such as the European Council, have imposed strict sanctions against the Republic of South Africa because of its system of apartheid.

Apartheid is a policy of racial segregation and political and economic discrimination. As practiced in South Africa it gives the white minority all power and privileges while denying power and privileges to the black majority.

Condemning South Africa

The Republic of South Africa, previously called the Union of South Africa, was formed in 1910. It was an uneasy coalition between the descendants of British settlers, Dutch settlers (known as Afrikaners), and the indigenous black population, who today make up 75 percent of the population. Strict segregation between the white ruling class and the black majority began early on, and the principles of apartheid ("apartness") were firmly in place by late 1940s. They include severe restrictions on interracial marriage, work, and educational opportunities, as well as housing, travel, voting, and other rights.

The UN has been condemning South African racial policies since 1946—strongly since 1960. In that year, apartheid was brought to world attention by the Sharpeville massacre, in which South African policemen fired on a group of unarmed black protestors. About 70 protestors were killed and another 190 were wounded. In 1977 South Africa, although still a member of the UN, was banned from all General Assembly activities. That same year the Security Council voted for a mandatory arms embargo against South Africa. Subsequent sanctions cut South Africa off from virtually all foreign investment, cultural exchange, international sports participation, and trade.

South Africa suffered considerably from this international boycott. Food prices and other indicators of inflation rose dramatically, the country's foreign debt rocketed, and many of its most qualified workers left the country in search of better

Finishing Lines

opportunities. Meanwhile, its domestic economy suffered also; at some points, almost 25 percent of the country's entire budget has been spent on security to maintain the apartheid laws. Simon Brand, chairman of the South African Development Bank, has said, "Apartheid is a monkey on the back of our economy. It is suffocating us."

Largely for this reason, the ruling government of South Africa has, in the last few years, begun easing its restrictive laws. A major breakthrough came in 1990 when President F.W. de Klerk lifted the laws concerning classification of races and

Vietnamese refugees, fleeing poverty and political repression, drift at sea awaiting rescue. Millions of refugees encounter similar hardships worldwide.

housing restrictions. That year de Klerk also legalized the banned African National Congress (ANC) party and released several political prisoners, including ANC spokesman Nelson Mandela, who had been imprisoned in 1963 under a life sentence.

Following these moves, the European Council and the United States slowly began easing their sanctions against South Africa. It is likely that the United Nations will follow. The situation in South Africa is still grim: violence is rampant, 25 percent of the population still owns 80 percent of the land, state schools are still segregated, and six times more money is spent on white schools than on black. But it appears that the sanctions imposed by the UN—isolating South Africa culturally, diplomatically, and economically—have played a direct role in reforming its racial policies. There is beginning to be a feeling among the international community that South Africa is on the mend.

Refugees

In addition to its other work, a major component of the UN's humanitarian efforts concerns refugees. The usual definition of a refugee is someone who has fled a home country, crossing international borders, to escape war, ethnic discrimination, religious persecution, or a brutal government. Sometimes people who are escaping economic hardship or environmental degradation are also considered refugees. In addition, there are an estimated twenty-three million displaced persons—refugees trapped in their own lands and unable to leave—around the world.

The current roster of large refugee populations includes Iraqi Kurds and Shiites fleeing the wrath of Iraqi leader Saddam Hussein, Ethiopians searching for relief from famine, Haitians and Vietnamese escaping poverty and political repression, Bangladeshis dispossessed by floods, and Serbs, Croats, and Bosnians finding shelter from age-old tribal feuds in the former Yugoslavia.

Both the sheer number of refugees and their general status have grown increasingly severe in recent years. In 1980 the UN identified eight million refugees worldwide. By 1991 that number had doubled. It is expected to double again by the year 2000. Jan Eliasson, the UN undersecretary general for humanitarian affairs, has said that the refugee situation "has emerged as one of the most pressing issues of the post-Cold War era."

Repatriation

Most refugees leave their home countries with only minimal supplies of clothing and food. For many years the role of the UN Office of the High Commissioner for Refugees (UNHCR) was simply to provide temporary shelter and food to these exiles. UNHCR has since expanded its duties to

Refugees from Bosnia-Herzegovina find safety and a place to sleep in a temporary shelter. The shelter was provided by the UNHCR, which is primarily concerned with providing shelter and food for exiles.

include helping refugees return, or repatriate, when it is safe or resettle in a new land if that becomes necessary.

These practices bring with them a raft of problems related to the long-term well-being of the refugees. Permanently returning an entire population to its homeland, especially when that country is unstable, is risky, expensive, time consuming, and complex. The task of resettling refugees in a new country creates a different set of problems and challenges, though they are often just as complex.

The UN has had some notable successes in returning refugees to their homes, such as in Afghanistan. Here, the biggest UN-assisted effort in history has helped more than a million refugees from warfare between a Soviet-backed government and Islamic warlords successfully return from temporary shelters in Pakistan.

An Afghan refugee family returns to their home country as part of a voluntary repatriation program assisted by the UN.

However, repatriation can also produce mixed results. One example is Cambodia. When Pol Pot's Khmer Rouge army was ousted by the Vietnamese in the early 1980s, it triggered a bloody war from which some 350,000 people fled. Ongoing battles among the three main factions (Khmer Rouge opposition guerrillas, the ruling Vietnam-backed Cambodian government, and a nationalist party led by former ruler Prince Sihanouk) have hindered UN efforts toward peace in the region.

Efforts in Cambodia

Still, the UN has had some success, notably in establishing a series of border camps and in supervising democratic elections. But life in the temporary camps is extremely difficult, and refugees are generally eager to leave them. Although some Cambodian refugees have been resettled overseas, the UN is overseeing a huge operation to repatriate most of them. As of late 1992, about 180,000 had returned home.

The program has succeeded in more ways than one. One aspect of the resettlement effort lies in providing refugees with cash or land and housing materials. This not only gives them the means to begin their lives again, but also helps strengthen the weak Cambodian economy. Repatriation is also helping Cambodia's faltering recovery in other ways. UN agencies have hired some former refugees while others have gone to work drilling new water wells and upgrading roads and railways.

But many observers feel that the results do not justify the tremendous expense. The UN operation in Cambodia is spending $3 billion annually for a relatively small number of refugees; in Afghanistan, which has ten times as many refugees, the UN spends only $100 million a year

Returning Cambodians build a house. In addition to transport and a year's supply of food, Cambodian returnees can choose between different forms of UN assistance, including a housing plot and housing kit.

on refugee aid.

These critics also point out that, after providing a degree of help in repatriating Cambodians, the UN has backed off from a full-scale effort to rebuild the nation. They fear that the UN's reluctance to finish the job it began builds false hope among Cambodians who have come to rely on UN aid for rebuilding their country. They say that greater resources and technical expertise, as well as a stronger role in long-term development, is needed.

Lain Guest, a senior fellow at the Refugee Policy Group in Washington, D.C., and a former UN official in Cambodia, has written that UNHCR has a "dread of being sucked into anything that remotely resembles 'development.' This has caused reintegration [repatriation] to stutter instead of soar. . . . UNHCR and donors must adopt a clear policy [toward repatriation], instead of flirting with the principle . . . and backing off from the practice."

Resettlement

When repatriation is impossible, due to continuing conflict or other reasons, refugees are sometimes permanently resettled in other countries. One example is the resettlement of a large number of Vietnamese in America. Many other countries have long histories of acting as compassionate hosts.

But integrating thousands of new arrivals into a nation creates its own set of problems in balancing compassion with practicality. Refugees may speak a different language, possess varying degrees of job skills, or have unfamiliar religions and customs. The arrival of massive numbers of new immigrants can trigger economic confusion and even violence in the host country. Recently, Germany has seen a resurgence of neo-Nazi violence linked, in part, with the arrival of large numbers of immigrants.

Neo-Nazis march in Germany to express their staunch opposition to the number of immigrants entering their country. This attitude complicates resettlement efforts.

One example of the problems in resettlement can be seen in the fallout of the ongoing warfare in the former Yugoslavia, where ethnic Serbs have been waging a bloody war against Muslim Bosnians. This war has created a massive refugee population, primarily Bosnians fleeing well-armed Serbian aggression.

In 1993, 1.6 million people in this region were being housed in temporary refugee centers, with thousands more arriving every week. Living conditions in these camps were primitive, especially in the dead of winter. There were also an estimated 1.3 million displaced persons—refugees living within Bosnia and unable to escape to the camps.

UNHCR has sought permanent homes for the Bosnians in more than twenty countries, but with little success. Virtually all the governments of these nations have been reluctant to take in the refugees permanently. One reason is that they

Croatians returning to their home show disbelief over its complete destruction. They are among the thousands of displaced persons in the former Yugoslavia who have no place to go.

Unable to comprehend the death and destruction caused by ethnic warfare in their country, refugees from Bosnia-Herzegovina sit speechless. UN agencies have had difficulty finding new homes for people such as these.

fear it would be seen as yielding to the Serbs, whose policy of ethnic cleansing, or the forced removal of non-Serbs from Serbian-dominated territory, would benefit from the permanent relocation of the Bosnians.

There is as yet no agreement among potential host countries on a formal policy or long-term plan for the Bosnians. Since these countries cannot agree among themselves, the UN's efforts at resettling the refugees have been stalled, in part, by the need to maintain cordial political ties between these countries. This effort to balance humanitarian concerns with the practical concerns of host nations will be a major challenge for the UN in the future. As Jean Noel Wetterwald, a spokesperson for UNHCR, recently stated, "You cannot ask us to keep solving problems if there is not the minimum of political consensus to stop them. We're doing what we can, but it's a drop in the ocean."

THEY SHALL BEAT THEIR SWORDS INTO
PLOWSHARES, AND THEIR SPEARS INTO
PRUNING HOOKS. NATION SHALL NOT LIFT
UP SWORD AGAINST NATION, NEITHER
SHALL THEY LEARN WAR ANY MORE

6

Finding a Niche for the Future

A new chapter in the history of the United Nations has begun. The machinery of the United Nations, which had often been rendered inoperative by the dynamics of the Cold War, is suddenly at the center of international efforts to deal with unresolved problems of the past decades as well as an emerging array of present and future issues.
—Boutros Boutros-Ghali,
Empowering the United Nations

(Opposite page) An inscription from the Bible on a wall at the United Nations Plaza eloquently describes the UN's goal of achieving world peace and cooperation between nations.

THE RECENT BREAKUP of the Soviet Union is changing the rules under which the UN operated for so long—rules governed by the cold war and the deep division between the superpowers. Some of these changes can already be seen, as the Security Council shakes off its longstanding paralysis and the General Assembly becomes increasingly assertive.

The UN's ability to undertake peacekeeping operations, for instance, has dramatically changed. In the four years following the Soviet breakup, the UN mounted as many peacekeeping operations as it did in the forty years before. The number of UN soldiers and police officers increased fourfold in the first half of 1992, swelling

89

to fifty thousand by the end of the year. The UN is also making unprecedented use of military force to carry out humanitarian aid in areas such as Bosnia and Somalia.

As journalist David Horsey noted early in 1992, "After 40 years of being rendered impotent, intractable and irrelevant by Cold War bellicosity and Third World verbosity, the UN finds itself in a new world order where the lofty goals [of its charter] may at last be in reach." One measure of this newfound effectiveness is that in 1988 UN peacekeeping forces were awarded the Nobel Prize for their efforts to achieve world peace.

This newfound power and effectiveness has taken many within the UN by surprise, creating a new set of complex problems. Alexander Watson,

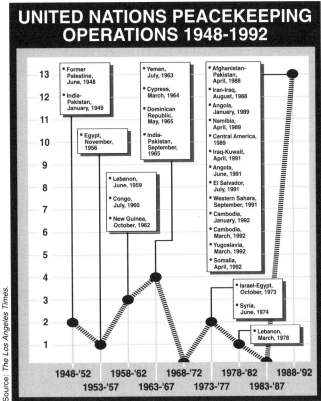

Source: The Los Angeles Times.

the U.S. deputy permanent representative to the UN, has likened the UN to a houseplant that languished in a basement for forty years, then was suddenly exposed to sunlight and told to "act like an oak": "Things are moving so fast, and people are so enthralled by the chance to solve problems at last without going to war, that we haven't made the adjustments necessary to understand what this will take."

Sharing the power

In 1992 alone, 13 new states, most of them newly independent provinces of the former Soviet Union, were admitted as members to the UN. This brings the total number of member states to 179. These new states, as well as the smaller nations who were already UN members, are vocal in their desire for more equal representation in all UN matters.

One of the most crucial issues for these new nations, and for other nations around the world, is the balance of power within the Security Council. The council's current arrangement—the five victors of World War II as the only permanent members—does not accurately reflect the realities of the world today.

Dozens of countries have gained independence and become new members since the UN's formation. Some nations, such as Brazil and Nigeria, have emerged to become economic and political leaders in their respective regions. The world's centers of power and influence are not as focused around Europe and the United States as they were in 1945. Journalist Horsey calls the present Security Council, which is still focused on these regions, "the biggest anachronism of all . . . the once-daunting five victors of the Second World War . . . devolved into one ex-superpower-turned-economic-basketcase, two faded European colonial powers, a Third World gerontocracy, and the single remaining superpower."

There are strong calls by many UN members to create a more evenly balanced council. Brazil and Nigeria are often mentioned as possible permanent members, since their presence would provide geographic diversity and reflect their regional importance. Some diplomats have also proposed adding Japan and Germany to reflect their current economic clout.

Unlike the council, the General Assembly gives each member nation equal weight in decision making. But there is a strong movement from within to give it a stronger role in the peacemaking process. General Assembly president Stoyan Gaven of Bulgaria put it matter-of-factly before the assembly in 1992: "There are maybe 100 situations in the world where the UN must react. Why [should it be] only the Security Council [that makes decisions]?"

The role of the United States

Even with the UN's efforts toward balancing internal power, the United States—as the world's only remaining superpower—will probably assume an increasingly dominant role in worldwide peacekeeping. This was true in Somalia, when the UN asked American forces to help restore order and resume humanitarian shipments after the UN's efforts had failed. America will probably also continue to be the strongest single presence in the UN's other activities.

Many diplomats and experts warn that the United States must be careful not to abuse this dominant role. No single government, they say, can hope to solve today's complex problems without international cooperation. Dr. Stanley Kalpage, the Sri Lankan ambassador to the UN, has stated, "What is necessary is that the demo-

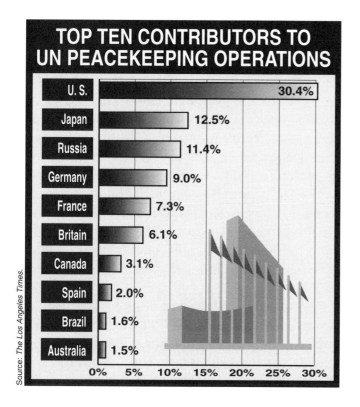

TOP TEN CONTRIBUTORS TO UN PEACEKEEPING OPERATIONS

Country	Percentage
U.S.	30.4%
Japan	12.5%
Russia	11.4%
Germany	9.0%
France	7.3%
Britain	6.1%
Canada	3.1%
Spain	2.0%
Brazil	1.6%
Australia	1.5%

0% 5% 10% 15% 20% 25% 30%

Source: *The Los Angeles Times.*

cratic process should operate. The U.S. must be sensitive to other cultures, to other points of view—consultative in its approach, ultimately dominant but not domineering."

One reason that the United States remains a dominant figure in the UN is that it is, far and away, the largest single contributor to the UN's finances, supplying nearly a quarter of its annual regular budget and a third of its peacekeeping budget. Many people feel that this financial inequality does not foster equal decision making. Journalist S. Nihal Singh of the *Hindustan Times* has written, "It is time to reform the UN. When one country, the US, pays a full 25% of [the total budget] . . . it is entitled to call the tune."

Restructuring the present system of dues payment would give the members of the UN a more equitable distribution of power. It could also provide the means to solve another major problem: getting members to pay on time.

Nearly every member state in the UN is chronically behind in its dues. The United States may be the UN's largest single contributor, but it is also the biggest overall debtor. President Clinton, early in his term, indicated a strong desire for America to "pay up, and pay up now" to maintain its credibility within the UN.

The UN's overall budget will almost certainly increase. The projected budget for world environmental protection alone is $125 billion a year, and peacekeeping operations during the first half of 1992 increased fourfold, from $700 million to $2.8 billion.

The chronic slowness in paying for this budget severely hampers the UN's ability to move quickly and efficiently and will be one of the biggest obstacles for the organization in the future. As Boutros Boutros-Ghali has noted, "At a time when the United Nations is being asked to do more than ever, it is being shortchanged by the member states who have breached their legal obligations. . . . The continued viability [and] credibility of the United Nations itself is threatened."

Strengthening the UN's peacekeeping force

For many, one of the UN's greatest failures has been its inability to maintain a permanent peacekeeping force—that is, a standing army that can quickly respond to crises. The UN charter calls for the formation of such a force, but it has never been organized. Instead, groups of "blue berets" and "blue helmets" have always been put together haphazardly as specific emergencies arose.

This piecemeal approach has hampered the UN's effectiveness as well as its credibility. Mark Sommer, a research associate in the Peace and Conflict Studies program at the University of California, Berkeley, recently wrote, "UN peacekeeping has always suffered from being an ad hoc affair in which nations voluntarily contribute troops from their own armed forces (and withdraw them whenever they choose), with little training in the highly specialized tasks of peacekeeping."

Many nations have been reluctant to place their troops directly under UN command and have been skeptical that a permanent UN force would treat all countries equitably all the time. Journalist P.S. Suryanrayana, writing in the Madras, India, paper *The Hindu* about the lack of a permanent force, observed:

> Over the years, it has become fashionable to blame the [UN's] failure . . . on the coldblooded politics of the cold-war period. But . . . the original plan did not take off [because] UN members have shown no inclination to place their soldiers under an external command for an indefinite period of time.

Boutros-Ghali is strongly in favor of restructuring UN peacekeeping operations to end this ad hoc nature. A flexible, always-available military force drawn from member nations, he argues, could act quickly and decisively in emergencies.

Finnish peacekeeping forces arrive in Namibia in 1989, as part of a UN plan to monitor elections in that country. The UN has been criticized for the often haphazard way in which troops are assembled when emergencies arise.

He proposes that this standing world police force should entail special units from member nations that would stay with their home armies until needed. Such forces, Boutros-Ghali notes, probably would not be enough "to deal with a threat from a major army equipped with sophisticated weapons. They would be useful, however, in meeting any threat posed by military force of a lesser order."

Responding with force

The make-up and readiness of UN peacekeeping forces could become even more important in the near future. In June 1993 the UN Security Council changed peacekeeping rules that allow UN troops to use force or firepower *only* when under attack. Under the new rules and in certain circumstances, aggressive action by UN forces is not only allowed, it is *required.*

This change came about after a June 5 ambush that killed twenty-three Pakistani peacekeepers in Somalia. UN officials blamed Somali clan leader Mohammed Farah Aidid for the ambush and responded by ordering UN troops to attack his strongholds. The assaults, launched on June 12 and 13, destroyed most of Aidid's weapons.

The UN action demonstrates the organization's ability to back its missions with military force. This could be important, UN officials believe, where a small group disrupts aid that the larger community wants and needs. Peacekeeping and humanitarian missions depend on the UN's ability to deliver what it promises. UN officials and some world leaders believe that unanswered attacks on UN peacekeepers could hurt future missions. However, this new, aggressive stance will probably be debated for many months.

In addition to dealing with issues affecting peacekeeping operations the UN will also need to

UN troops were ordered to attack the strongholds of Somali clan leader Mohammed Farah Aidid (right).

A nuclear weapons test leaves behind an ominous cloud. Although East-West tensions have eased with the end of the cold war and the Soviet Union's collapse, nuclear disarmament remains a concern for the UN.

address the long-term questions of disarmament and, especially, of nuclear weapons.

The threat of nuclear war between the superpowers, a primary fear during the cold war, was a huge factor in post-World War II global politics. In 1961, speaking to the General Assembly, President John F. Kennedy summed up the world's feelings when he said:

> Today every inhabitant of this planet must contemplate the day when this planet will no longer be habitable. Every man, woman, and child lives under the nuclear sword of Damocles, hanging by the slenderest of threads, capable of being cut at any moment by accident or miscalculation or by madness. The weapons of man must be abolished before they abolish us.

The creation of the International Atomic Energy Agency had been one of the UN's first acts. It was designed to implement international control of nuclear weapons, but it was powerless to stop a huge increase in the arms race between the United States and the Soviet Union in the years following World War II. Meanwhile, several other countries, including India, China, and France, also developed nuclear weapons. Currently, several countries, including Pakistan, Iraq, and Israel, are thought to be working on developing nuclear weapons of their own.

Although conventional and chemical weapons are still a large factor in the $900 billion spent every year worldwide on arms and troops, nuclear weapons are the single biggest issue in disarmament. The breakup of the Soviet Union has reduced the nuclear threat somewhat, but roughly fifty thousand nuclear weapons still exist worldwide; in particular, the future of the nuclear weapons of the Soviet Union and in the volatile countries of the Middle East is unclear.

Progress toward control has been extremely slow. Significant milestones include the Nuclear Test Ban Treaty of 1963 and the more recent Strategic Arms Limitation Talks (SALT) and Strategic Arms Reduction Talks (START). The UN has played a major role in these talks and in clarifying the complex issues that arise when a country feels it needs nuclear arms to defend itself.

The UN's commitment to removing the nuclear threat from the globe is a major challenge for the future. Israeli diplomat Abba Eban summed up the prevailing attitude in an address to the General Assembly in 1965. The UN's strong emphasis "on the pacific [peaceful] settlement of disputes," he said, "is not only a reaction to the nuclear peril. It is inspired by hope as well as fear."

Avoiding the mistakes of the past

In "An Agenda for Peace" Boutros-Ghali, like Santayana, suggests that we must learn from the mistakes of the past if we are to avoid repeating them. He writes movingly of the future direction he would like to see the United Nations Organization take under his guidance:

> The nations and peoples of the United Nations are fortunate in a way that those of the League of Na-

President John F. Kennedy signs the Nuclear Test Ban Treaty in 1963, an important step toward nuclear disarmament.

tions were not. We have been given a second chance to create the world of our Charter that they were denied. With the cold war ended we have drawn back from the brink of a confrontation that threatened the world and, too often, paralyzed our Organization.

Even as we celebrate our restored possibilities, there is a need to ensure that the lessons of the past four decades are learned and that the errors, or variations of them, are not repeated. For there may not be a third opportunity for our planet which, now for different reasons, remains endangered. . . .

A conviction has grown, among nations large and small, that an opportunity has been regained to achieve the great objectives of the Charter—a United Nations capable of securing justice and human rights and promoting, in the words of the Charter, "social progress and better standards of life in larger freedom." This opportunity must not be squandered. The Organization must never again be crippled as it was in the era that has now passed.

The UN General Assembly, where hopes for global peace, prosperity, and stability may one day come to fruition.

Appendix I

Membership

United Nations membership is open to all nations that accept and are able and willing to carry out the obligations of the charter. Prospective members must be recommended by the Security Council and accepted by a two-thirds vote of the General Assembly.

Suspension of membership or expulsion may be invoked by the Security Council. The council has a similar power to restore membership. Certain nonmember states, such as Switzerland and the Holy See (the Vatican state), are allowed to maintain permanent observers at the United Nations. In addition, a great many nongovernment organizations (NGOs), such as the International Red Cross, the Boy and Girl Scouts, and Amnesty International, maintain permanent or semipermanent observers.

Appendix II

Structure

The United Nations is divided into six principal parts: the General Assembly, the Security Council, the Economic and Social Council, the Trusteeship Council, the International Court of Justice, and the Secretariat.

1. The General Assembly is the main body of the UN. It is composed of representatives from all the member states. Each has one vote. Decisions on important matters require a two-thirds majority; decisions on other matters require only a simple majority.

The General Assembly's regular session begins annually in the autumn and usually lasts about two months. In addition it may meet in special sessions or in special emergency sessions. A new president is elected each year, rotating among five groups of states (African, Asian, Eastern European, Latin American, and Western European and other states) to ensure geographical representation.

To deal with the hundreds of separate agenda items in each session, the General Assembly is divided into seven main committees: disarmament and international security; economic and financial; social, humanitarian, and cultural; decolonization; administrative and budgetary; legal; and special political considerations.

Some questions are dealt with only by special committee; others by plenary sessions (meetings of the assembly as a whole). Decisions of the General Assembly have no legally binding force, but world opinion adds weight to General Assembly decisions.

2. The Security Council is responsible for the maintenance of global peace and security. It has fifteen

members: five permanent members (People's Republic of China, France, Russia, the United Kingdom, and the United States) and ten rotating members, which are elected by the General Assembly for two-year terms.

Each member has one vote. Decisions on major issues require nine votes and must include all five permanent members. The council operates continuously, and representatives are present at UN headquarters at all times. The Security Council's decisions, unlike those of the General Assembly, are legally binding.

3. The Economic and Social Council coordinates the UN's specialized agencies for economic and social work and consults with more than one thousand NGOs that are active within those spheres. It has fifty-four members, who each serve three-year terms.

Voting is by simple majority, with one vote per member. The council holds two regular sessions each year, one in New York and one in Geneva, each lasting about one month. Year-round work is carried out by subcommissions and committees, which report to the council at regular meetings.

4. The Trusteeship Council supervises the administration of trust territories and oversees their development toward self-government or independence. Most of the original trust territories, which were primarily in Africa and the Pacific, have gained independence since the council was formed in 1945, and the number of council members has declined. Its members currently are the same states as those of the Security Council, with the United States acting as the only administering state for the only remaining trusteeship, the Pacific Islands. The council meets annually, usually midyear, and holds special sessions when required.

5. The International Court of Justice oversees international conventions, customs, and laws. Any UN member may bring a case before it, and a nonmember may do so as well if recommended by the Security Council and General Assembly. The court's fifteen judges are elected by the General Assembly and Security Council, with care taken

to ensure that the principal legal systems of the world are represented. No two judges may be citizens of the same nation. Each serves a term of nine years and may be reelected. The court is headquartered at the Hague, in the Netherlands.

6. The Secretariat is the administrative arm of the UN. At its head is the secretary-general, who is appointed by the General Assembly on the recommendation of the Security Council. The first secretary-general was Trygvie Lie, of Norway, who served until 1953. The second was Dag Hammarskjöld, of Sweden, who served from 1953 until 1961. The third was U Thant, of Burma, who served from 1961 to 1971. The fourth was Kurt Waldheim, of Austria, who served from 1972 to 1981. The fifth was Javier Pérez de Cuéllar, of Peru, who served from 1982 to 1991. The sixth is Boutros Boutros-Ghali, of Egypt, who took office in 1992. The Secretariat carries out the day-to-day work at UN headquarters in New York and at related offices around the world. The Secretariat is, in effect, an international civil service. Its employees are required to represent only the UN, not any outside government or authority. Among their many duties are administering peacekeeping operations; organizing conferences, studies, and surveys; interpreting speeches and translating documents; and supplying the public with information about the UN.

Organizations
to Contact

The best source of additional information on the United Nations is the organization itself. The UN maintains two offices that are devoted to supplying the public with information about its activities. In addition, the UN offers guided tours of its headquarters in New York City.

UN Public Inquiries Unit—Public Services Section
United Nations
New York, NY 10017
(212) 963-4475

UN Information Center
1889 F St.
Washington, DC 20006
(202) 289-8670

Guided UN Tours
Group Program Unit
Room GA-56
United Nations
New York, NY 10017
(212) 963-7539

Guided tours are given in English daily except on Christmas and New Year's Day, every half hour from 9:00 A.M. to 4:45 P.M. The tour lasts about one hour. For groups of fifteen or more, call (212) 963-4440, for reservations. Meetings of the UN's various committees and councils are sometimes open to the public. Tickets are available on a first-come, first-serve basis. For meeting schedules, call (212) 963-7113 on the day of your visit.

Suggestions for Further Reading

Basic Facts about the UN. New York: United Nations Organization, 1987.

Andrew Boyd, *Fifteen Men on a Powder Keg: A History of the Security Council*. New York: Stein & Day, 1971.

Clark M. Eichenberger, *UN: The First Twenty-Five Years*. New York: Harper & Row, 1970.

Cornelia Meigs, *The Great Design: Men and Events in the UN 1945-1963*. Boston: Little, Brown, 1964.

Works Consulted

Anna-Christine d'Adesky, "UNHCR: Facing the Refugee Challenge," *UN Chronicle*, September 1991.

K.M. Amladi, "How Other Nations Suffer and Cope," *World Press Review*, January 1992.

Benjamin Barber, "Jihad vs. McWorld," *The Atlantic*, March 1992.

Peter Berle, "Charting a Sustainable Course," *Audubon*, January 1991.

Ray Bonner, "Why We Went," *Mother Jones*, March/April 1993.

Boutros Boutros-Ghali, "Empowering the United Nations," *Foreign Affairs*, Winter 1992-93.

"Caring for Refugees" (interview with) Sadako Ogata, *World Press Review*, July 1991.

John Clements and Diana Silimperi, "Immunizing the Children of Poverty," *World Health*, March/April 1991.

Pamela Constable, "At War's End in El Salvador," *Current History*, March 1993.

Robert Cullan, "Human Rights Quandary," *Foreign Affairs*, Winter 1992.

Basil Davidson, "Apartheid: The Shameful Record," *UNESCO Courier*, May/June 1986.

Frederick Freksa, *A Peace Congress of Intrigue: Vienna, 1815*. New York: Century, 1919.

Peter Haas, "Appraising the Earth Summit," *Environment*, October 1992.

James Henry, "Growing Nowhere: South Africa's Economic Crisis," *New Republic*, August 20, 1990.

Charles Hopkins, "From Awareness to Action," *UNESCO Courier*, July 1991.

John Keagan, "Is South Africa Invulnerable?" *U.S. News & World Report*, March 23, 1987.

Wilfried Kreisel, "Environmental Health in the 1990s," *World Health*, January/February 1990.

Paul Lewis, "Peacekeeper Is Now a Peacemaker," *The New York Times*, January 25, 1993.

Paul Lewis, "UN Says Somalis Must Disarm Before Peace," *The New York Times*, December 6, 1992.

Eugene Linden, "Rio's Legacy," *Time*, June 22, 1992.

Catherine Lumby, "A Poor Record on Human Rights," *World Press Review*, April 1992.

Sally Marks, *The Illusion of Peace: International Relations in Europe 1918-33*. New York: St. Martin's Press, 1976.

Bruce Nelan, "Today, Somalia. . . .", *Time*, December 21, 1992.

Harold Nicolson, *The Congress of Vienna: A Study in Allied Unity*. New York: Harcourt, Brace, 1946.

Karen Pennar, "Will the Embargo Work?" *Business Week*, September 17, 1990.

Carla Anne Robbins, "Into the Breach," *U.S. News & World Report*, June 29, 1992.

Bruce Russett and James Sutterlin, "The UN in a New World Order," *Foreign Affairs*, Spring 1991.

Daniel Santiago, "The Peace Process in El Salvador," *America*, January 11, 1992.

William Shawcross, "Cambodia: the UN's Biggest Gamble," *Time*, December 28, 1992.

George Slocombe, *A Mirror to Geneva*. New York: Henry Holt, 1938.

James Stevenson, "Food for Naught," *New Republic*, September 21, 1992.

James Torrans, "El Salvador Report Card," *America*, October 24, 1992.

Sir Charles Webster, *The Congress of Vienna*. Reprint. Lanham, Maryland: Barnes and Noble, 1963.

Yearbook of the United Nations. New York: United Nations Organization, 1991.

Index

About the Author

Adam Woog is a free-lance writer whose articles have appeared in many magazines and newspapers in the United States, Asia, and Europe. He is a former staff writer for the *Seattle Times* and currently reviews books for that newspaper.

Woog often writes about his native Pacific Northwest. He is the author of *Sexless Oysters and Self-Tipping Hats: One Hundred Years of Invention in the Pacific Northwest,* which won the 1991 award for nonfiction history from the Washington Press Association, and *Atomic Marbles and Branding Irons: A Guidebook to Museums, Special Collections, and Roadside Curiosities in Washington and Oregon.* Both are published by Sasquatch Books.

Woog lives with his wife and daughter in Seattle, Washington.

Picture Credits

Cover photo by © Dennis Hallinan 1991/FPG

Amnesty International, 72, 75

AP/Wide World Photos, 34, 56

The Bettmann Archive, 10, 14, 26, 28

CARE Photo, 62

Deutschland Erwacht/Simon Wiesenthal Center Archives, Los Angeles, CA, 29

FAO Photo by F. Botts, 71

Library of Congress, 13, 21, 35

Los Alamos National Laboratory, 97

National Archives, 17, 20, 30, 32

North Wind Picture Archives, 16

Reuters/Bettmann, 46, 57, 58, 60, 65, 96

UN Photo/J.K. Issac, 6, 52

UN Photo/M. Grant, 8, 95, 99

UN Photo/M. Tzovaras, 66

UN Photo/Marcel Bolomey, 40

UN Photo/P. Sudahkaran, 49

UN Photo/Peter Magubane, 9

UNESCO/Michèle Spinelli, 67

UNHCR/A. Hollmann, 81, 86, 87

UNHCR/D. Bregnard, 76

UNHCR/I. Avest, 53

UNHCR/K. Gooi, 84

UNHCR/M. Elkhoury, 82

UNHCR/P. Deloche, 80

UNITED NATIONS, 36, 38, 39, 42, 48, 50, 74, 88, 98

UPI/Bettmann, 19, 22, 23, 24, 25, 44, 45, 51

WFP/FAO photo by P. Vaughan-Whitehead, 64

WFP/FAO photo by G. Tortoli, 68

WHO photo by P. Merchez, 70

WHO photo by P. Wolmuth, 85